Jeannette presents refreshing and unique insights into "our pilgrim journey" on this planet Earth. Her refreshing wit and winsome candor, combined with a unique insight into biblical truth, will better prepare us for our journey. How good it is to know as pilgrims in this land that our traveling has a final destination.

—Cliff Barrows, Program and
Music Director for the Billy Graham team

Jeannette Clift George's book *Travel Tips from a Reluctant Traveler* is filled with warmth, love, and, of course, wonderful humor. She has the gift of wrapping spiritual gems in humor. It is very much like having a deep and thoughtful conversation with the author, which is always a profit and a pleasure.

—Dr. Louis Evans, Minister, National
Presbyterian Church, Washington, D.C.,
and Colleen Townsend Evans, Author of
A *Deeper Joy*

I love the book! It's full of wisdom and humor and . . . details . . . our search for faith with clarity and simplicity.

—Julie Harris, Actress

Joyce and I have enjoyed our "trip of life" together. It indeed is Jesus who makes the trip worthwhile. We are inspired by the gifts of wit, charm, and insight given to Jeannette Clift George to help enhance our journey all the more. The transparency in her own journey is refreshing and provides hope that you, too, can successfully reach your desired destination on your spiritual trip.

—Dr. and Mrs. Adrian Rogers,
Bellevue Baptist Church, Memphis,
Tenn., President of the Southern
Baptist Convention

With a combination of humor and depth, Jeannette Clift George gives us an inside view of her own spiritual journey in *Travel Tips from a Reluctant Traveler*. Charmingly written, [this book] captures the essence of what it means to know the Lord personally and walk with him daily in the busy, frenzied life of being a producer, director, playwright, author, actress, and wife.

Like Rosalind Russell's *Life Is a Banquet*, [*Travel Tips*] keeps you laughing heartily, yet deeply moved. Jeannette tells you how to hang on to biblical principles when you'd rather stop the world and get off. Read this book. It's great. Then see the movie too. You'll love them both.

—Luci Swindoll,
Author of *You Bring the Confetti*

Jeannette Clift George combines her rare gift of communication, humor, and imagination with the insight of an authentic believer on a real journey. She has a sharp eye for the masks all actors wear and a refreshing candor about her own journey with which all of us as fellow travelers can identify. Combining wit and insight, she has a deep reverence for the Word of God and for the One who says, "I am the road, the truth, and the life."

—Jimmy R. Allen, President, ACTS
satellite network

Each of us has experienced delays and frustrations, not only in our journey from New York to Chicago, but also, as Jeanette so aptly reminds us, in our continuous journey through life. Many readers will identify with Jeannette's experiences, as I did, and will find their journey more joyful because of the universal truths of her travel tips.

—Millie Dienert, International
Prayer Chairman, Amsterdam 1983, 1986

TRAVEL TIPS FROM A RELUCTANT TRAVELER

TRAVEL TIPS FROM A RELUCTANT TRAVELER

JEANNETTE CLIFT GEORGE

Publishers since 1798

THOMAS NELSON PUBLISHERS
Nashville • Camden • Kansas City

Published in Nashville, Tennessee, by Thomas Nelson, Inc., and
distributed in Canada by Lawson Falle, Ltd., Cambridge, Ontario.

Printed in the United States of America.

Scripture quotations are from THE NEW KING JAMES VERSION.
Copyright © 1979, 1980, 1982, Thomas Nelson, Inc., Publishers.

Scripture quotations noted NASB are from the New American
Standard Bible, © The Lockman Foundation 1960, 1962, 1963,
1968, 1971, 1972, 1973, 1975, 1977.

Scripture quotations noted Phillips are from J. B. Phillips: THE
NEW TESTAMENT IN MODERN ENGLISH, Revised Edition.
© J. B. Phillips 1958, 1960, 1972. Used by permission
of Macmillan Publishing Co., Inc.

Library of Congress Cataloging-in-Publication Data

George, Jeannette Clift.
    Travel tips from a reluctant traveler.

    1. Christian life—1960–   .   2. George, Jeannette
Clift.   I. Title.
BV4501.2.G43   1987   248.4   87–18423
ISBN 0-8407-4218-5

To the kneeling army of friends who consistently pray for me

PASSPORT

The Secretary of State
of the United States of America
hereby requests all whom it may concern to permit the citizen/
national of the United States named herein to pass
without delay or hindrance and in case of need to
give all lawful aid and protection.

NAME	BIRTHPLACE
Jeannette Clift George	Houston, TX
BIRTH DATE	**SIZE**
Many years ago	Frequently 16

OCCUPATION
Wife, Manager/Director of A.D. Players, Writer, Actress, Platform speaker

DISTINGUISHING MARKS
Furrowed brow, white knuckles, twenty minutes late

HUSBAND
Lorraine M. George

OCCUPATION
Construction Businessman; man of great wisdom; looks a little like Spencer Tracy

REFERENCES
A.D. Players, a Christian theater company based in Houston, Texas. Its annual season includes five major productions in Grace Theater as well as touring units performing a repertory of over twenty plays and offering full productions of Christian plays and musicals in various theaters throughout the world.

REDEMPTION CERTIFICATE
John 3:16

Foreword

*E*ven as she tells us of her reluctance to travel through this territory called life, Jeannette Clift George manages to make us want to drop what we are doing and climb aboard the "JCG Express"! Her infectious warmth and disarming humor allow each of us to identify immediately with the dilemmas she so transparently relates and to empathize readily with the familiar and human responses we have all experienced.

This phenomenally creative and godly woman has the ability to articulate what many of us have felt and thought in those situations that Paul assures us in 1 Corinthians 10:13 are so "common to man." Although the experiences and feelings may be "common," Jeannette's recounting of them is anything but common. In fact, she has a remarkably uncommon ability to elicit from her readers that nod and smile of recognition as we remember "I know what that feels like . . . I've been there before."

Without question, it is Jeannette's absolute confidence in her Lord that accounts for the spirit of celebration she so emphatically recommends to each of us. She has an uncanny knack for ferreting out and identifying with the humanness of biblical characters who have encouraged her because they were less than perfect. From the diverse lives of men like Naaman, Jonah, and Joshua, she has learned and shares with us lessons about being precisely who God intended for us to be—nothing more or less.

From the very beginning of her book, when she so hilariously empathizes with a terrified cat flying through space, to her simple explanation at the end of her book of why she is able to be patient and loving with people—"I've been a person for a long time"—Jeannette is joyous, living proof of Jesus' words in John 12:32: "If I be lifted up, I will draw all men to me."

You'll not be able to read this delightful book without becoming more familiar with the Lord this gifted author loves and serves with her whole heart.

—Dr. H. Edwin Young, Pastor
Second Baptist Church,
Houston, Tex.

CONTENTS

ONE

Examine Your
Preboarding Information

My cousins live in Asheville, North Carolina, where Jesse is a prominent surgeon. He is a fine man, a very gracious man, a very loving man, but a man who doesn't like cats. His wife, Frances, is a delightful person who loves cats.

One day, a little neighbor girl ran crying to their house. Her cat had climbed up in a tall, slender tree and couldn't get down. Jesse thought that was a very good place for a cat to be, but following Frances's gentle persuasion, he said, "Let's see what we can do to help."

The two of them decided that Frances, who is of diminutive stature, would grab the lower part of the tree and work it down until the topmost branches reached Jesse. Then Jesse, who is quite tall, would scoop the frightened cat from the top of the tree to safety. Their plan worked well at first. Frances grabbed the part of the tree within her reach and pulled it toward her. The tree tipped down like a thirsty giraffe, bearing a tiny passenger on its head. The branches were almost to Jesse when Frances lost her grip!

Whoom! The tree slipped from Frances's hands and sprang away with such great force that the cat was flung into space! Catapulted! Claws out! Eyes wide! Approaching a certain but unknown destiny.

The little girl was crushed, but the shock of her beloved cat's mode of departure stopped her sobbing. Frances was overcome by guilt because she and Jesse had lost the little girl's cat. Jesse tried not to laugh. They all accepted the foiled rescue attempt. What else could they do?

A few days later, Frances was in the grocery store and noticed a friend pushing a grocery cart with cat food in it. She knew that her friend's husband didn't like cats any more than Jesse did. "I see you have cat food. Do you have a cat?" she asked.

Her friend stopped, looked around to be sure no one else could hear, and said, "Frances, the strangest thing happened. My husband and I were sitting in our backyard when all of a sudden, out of nowhere, this cat landed at our feet! My husband looked at the cat and then at me. He said, 'Maude, the Lord has sent us a cat!'"

My cousins' story gives me new insight into the dilemmas of traveling and the bewilderments I often find in life. I identify with that cat! Often flung out into unchartered space, I'm not sure where I'm going, but I'm going there very rapidly. Clashing priorities, scrambled agenda, sudden assignments, unexpected incidents catapult me into areas and activities for which I have no comfortable preparation. Sometimes, I even look like that cat. Claws out! Eyes wide! Gasping for breath and trying unsuccessfully to get my act together before I land.

One such incident happened several years ago when I faced "minor surgery." Everyone assured me that it would be minor, and I adopted the word in order to maintain a rational dialogue. However, nothing in me agreed with the casualness of the term. The day before the operation, many smiling, healthy friends came to see me in the hospital. One of them, Dorothy, said, "I was back in my office two days after I had this same operation."

That helped. It gave me a proven frame of reference. I could visualize a time when everything would be all right, and I could join that loving army of sympathizers who proclaimed the operation as minor.

The operation was right on schedule. A few hours afterward, the surgeon paid one pleasant but perfunctory visit to my hospital room, and I was released the next afternoon. I was delighted by the good report, relieved to have the incident behind me, and eager to get back to my usual activities, so I went home to spend a day resting before I assumed the high gear of my usual activities.

One thing bothered me. I felt awful! The doctor had said I could do anything I felt like doing. He didn't know that by noon of the next day I felt like scratching off the smile he had worn while administering so inane a counsel. Anything I felt like doing, indeed! My head swam when I began to "feel like" getting dressed. My knees buckled when I looked at my shoes.

I remembered Dorothy's happy encouragement. According to her schedule, I would be back at work the next morning, yet I didn't feel like combing my hair for visitors. Only my imagination was vigorous. Something must be dreadfully wrong! Obviously, my minor surgery had been turned over to a novice surgeon who wanted to try his hand at the real thing before signing up for medical school. The rest of me was as limp as a trampled daisy.

Late that night, after a day spent in frantic attempts at instant recovery, I called Dorothy. "I'm not doing well at all," I moaned. "You were back at work in two days, and I don't think I'll make it in a week."

She was sympathetic, a good friend who hurt when I hurt. She was also truthful. "Jeannette, I was back at work in two days, but I fainted twice and had to be taken home."

Ohhh! The weakness was natural. It was going to be all right but not necessarily easy. Having been relieved of the responsibility for doing the impossible, which was to get well in an instant, I could direct my energies to a more rational and healthy recovery.

Such insights have often come during difficult experiences in my life, and throughout this book I'll share these travel tips like the writer of any good travel book, tips from a reluctant traveler whose experience might be much like yours.

Travel Tip:
Relieve yourself of the responsibility of doing the impossible. That is God's special prerogative.

This book is written from the viewpoint of a Christian life that hasn't always been easy. While others relaxed into a pattern of rhapsodic peace following their conversion, I did not. While others were given complete attitudinal changes with their packaged halos, I was not. While others moved joyously into their divinely appointed maturity, my travel was more reluctant.

Let's go back to the beginning of my journey. As is true

of many others, my path toward the narrow gate was not straight; it meandered and wandered, partly because I doubted my personal validity.

I've always wanted to be someone different from who I am. Someone better. There's a line in Christopher Fry's *The Lady's Not for Burning* where Alizon says, "Now I begin to be altogether different I suppose." As a child and as a young woman, I hoped that some sudden change was going to happen that would make me become what I wanted to be.

When I went away to college, I was sure that it would happen. I would become altogether different. When I came home, I was altogether the same as I had been when I went off to college—a little heavier, but the same person. It was difficult for me to realize that a *sudden* change was just not to happen.

I went to New York City to become the "World's Greatest Actress." I was going through a very bewildering personal time, and I *verbally* rejected everything I had been taught within the precious orientation of my Christian family. I was interested in philosophy, and I identified with any group that was searching for the truth. In fact, I was an existentialist until I met one. "Searching" seemed smart. Finding an answer wasn't the issue; it was the search that mattered.

During this time, I began to do exactly what I'd wanted to do all my life—act. I'm very shy. I'm a stammerer. I'm allergic to makeup. My eyes are funny, so I can't tell when I'm in the light and not in the light. It's very difficult for me to remember lines. So, of course, I'm an actress! What else would I be? All my life I thought if I could ever act in theater, I'd have everything I could ever want.

Once I began to have some continuity of performance and to receive recognition, a most bewildering thing happened: I wasn't satisfied. I became deeply depressed.

17

The good things happening in my life only served to highlight an unresolved personal dilemma. You see, I'd spent my life trying to be whatever the group around me wanted me to be. If people thought I was sweet, I tried to be sweet. If they thought I was funny, I tried to be funny. If they thought I was smart, I had to peddle harder, but I tried to fulfill their expectations. I was desperately, desperately trying to earn acceptance by pretending to be what I thought was expected of me. I had no way out, and there was no way for help to get to me. Only the uninitiated try to cure depression with logic like this: "If you are successful, why are you depressed?" My depression was evidenced by success that was not satisfying.

I thought the trick was to act as if I had it all together and everything would be fine. I didn't know enough to cry out, "HELP!" It was dreadful. I was suicidal. It was part of the pattern of my childhood to go to church, so I looked there. I visited a building that called itself a church, and after the service, as I went out of the sanctuary, I spoke to an usher who was standing near the door. I said, "I'm all alone in the city."

He shook my hand and muttered a brief greeting. Then he quickly handed me off to a woman who led me toward a group of people. "We always like visitors to take a tour of the church," she said, motioning toward the group. "Then you'll feel at home here."

I took her suggestion and followed the group through the church. After touring the prayer chapel, the offices, and other parts of the church, we went up to see the bell tower.

I remember standing there and thinking, I'm suicidal, and they take me up to see the bell tower? I knew I shouldn't be there, but the people hadn't taken the time to learn my problem, they had just motioned me through their "new member orientation."

Incidentally, don't blame people for not carrying your problem as a top priority on their agenda. We depressives often expect the world to stop and treat our pain. Sometimes God directs the world to be indifferent so we may see His love make the difference. That's exactly what happened to me.

Somebody who knew I was interested in literature sent me a trio of newly published books. One of those was the Phillips translation of the New Testament. I didn't know it was the Bible. Phillips doesn't say BIBLE on the cover, so I read it. I would carry it with me, and occasionally, somebody would recognize it and say, "Oh, you're reading the Bible."

And I'd say, "No, I don't read the Bible. I grew out of that."

And the person would say, "Well, that's the Bible."

"No, it isn't," I'd insist. "The Bible is a very old book, and this is a new book. It was written by an English scholar."

"Well, that is the Bible. Jeannette, you're reading the Epistles!"

"Don't fake me, man. I know about the Epistles," I said. "There were twelve of them. They followed Christ everywhere. This is a collection of letters. It starts off 'Dear So and So,' signed Paul."

Sometime during my reading, I got to the twelfth chapter of the book of Romans. Finally, I understood I was not in an ordinary book. It was God's Book. And a little phrase spoke to my deepest need: "Don't let the world squeeze you into its mold."[1] I read it with my initials on it.

My depression was probably the most realistic reaction I had to the circumstances of a life dedicated to be what everyone else wanted it to be. Here was a verse that said, "Don't do *that*. Be." I remember very logically dialoguing with whoever God might be. I said, "I can't be me. Nobody knowing me would want me."

God led me to another verse: "But God demonstrates His own love toward us, in that *while we were still sinners*, Christ died for us."[2] I remembered what I had been taught as a child, and I knew God knew everything there was to know about me. If God, knowing everything there was to know about me, died for me, He wasn't going to be shocked when He found out what I was really like. I cried out to God, holding that little Bible out, to remind Him of His promise. "All right, Jesus Christ! Whoever You are, You take over."

I didn't have the vaguest notion of what the Christian life was going to be like. I didn't know Jesus Christ in His deity. All I knew was one simple thing: What I was looking for couldn't be found anyplace else. So I said, "Here's my life. You take over."

The next morning I repeated the error I'd made so many times as a child: I expected to be altogether different. I could hardly wait to get to the mirror. I knew I'd be thinner. There was no doubt about *that*. I'd hoped that I'd have naturally curly blonde hair. I looked in the mirror, and I bore an astonishing resemblance to the way I'd looked the day before. It disturbed me. I thought, *Well, maybe it happens later*. I went to work and tried to be rhapsodic, but I couldn't.

Have you ever tried to joy? Tried to joy all by yourself? "I will joy, no matter what happens. Regardless of the circumstance, regardless of the way I feel, I'm going to joy." It's hard to do because it's impossible. (Later, as I read Scripture, I realized that joy is not *my* responsibility. Joy is God's responsibility. My responsibility is obedience. To my surprise, I've found that joy is always the result of obedience.)

I was very bewildered. I would go to people and say, "I

gave my life to Jesus Christ, but I think He gave it back because nothing happened." They told me that I didn't have enough faith. So I tried to have more faith. I'd go to my room, and I'd try to look like those people looked when they said it. (I hadn't learned that if you don't have the fact of faith, the look of faith doesn't make any difference. So I worked on the look I'd seen in others.) Their faces were perfectly calm until they got to the word *faith*. Then many magic and muscular things happened to their faces. They said, "Jeannette, what you need is more *faith*," and their eyebrows shot up to where I assumed halos were rooted. Their eyes rolled to indicate a heavenly attitude. Apparently, the activated halos caused tension because their voices became breathy and high-pitched. Oh, how I wanted to have just as severe a case of faith.

I figured it began with muscles at the back of the neck. "I'm going to have *faith*." Up went the eyebrows. "Faith." Back tossed the head. "Faith." Out with the chin. I practiced. The furrowed forehead. The tension in the scalp line. Nothing. I had a headache but no faith!

I've learned that this sad agenda is often followed by the newly converted. We hold our feelings responsible for information we haven't yet assimilated. But God doesn't abandon us to the morass of this malady. God's garden is not a maze that would block our every turn while He looks on in condescending amusement. Not only has He gone out of His way to bring us to Him, He has gone out of His way to help us live out what He has so effectively lived in. He has given us a Guidebook essential to our travels. It says, "Faith comes by hearing, and hearing by the Word of God."[3]

As I read the Bible during those next months, I learned that none of the great patriarchs became wise and faithful overnight. Take Moses, the man who led the Hebrew nation out of bondage in Egypt to the borders of the

Promised Land. He spent forty years in the desert before God used him to deliver His people. There in the desert, he was in process. Reading his story, I learned another travel tip.

Travel Tip:
Don't shortcut the process.

Frequently, most of us want to shortcut the process. A dear friend of mine sought to claim the kingdom of heaven with energetic persistence. Every godly speaker or focused preacher got her immediate attention. She made so many decisions for Christ that her commitment card was photocopied and her path to the altar worn to a faded strand. But each upbeat had a devastating downbeat. She wore herself out trying to be born again. One day we were talking on the phone, and she again began her story of woebegone wanderings. "Nothing worked," she admitted.

I'm still stunned by my comments to her. I said, "Your trouble isn't a lack of salvation; it's a lack of knowledge. Stop struggling for birth. You're born! Start growing up!" I held my breath after my outburst. How would she respond to such arrogance on my part?

With gentle laughter! She said, "You may be right. I'll look into that." And she did. In the next years, she grew like the well-seeded flower she truly was. My friend needed to direct her persistence to process. Many of us fail to celebrate in our travels throughout life because we deny the process.

Faith is a gift, a wonderful "Happy Birthday, Celebrate Forever" gift. But it is also a muscle. It must be exercised, and that happens through a lifelong process. God may take us in His grace from Monday to Friday, but we'll go through Tuesday, Wednesday, and Thursday to get there. These days, you can be sure, will be packed full of choices and deliberations, losings and winnings, all sorts of events that will be part of the processing of our week. Even though I have been a reluctant traveler, I can vouch for the certainty of God's unwavering fellowship, the sovereign promise of His itinerary, and His limitless patience with people in process.

Travel Tip:

Remind yourself in flight, it *is* going to be all right but not necessarily easy.

TWO

Protect the Integrity
of the Journey

Many years ago I visited the Steuben glass works in Corning, New York, and I watched the process of making glass through the window that surrounded the workshop. I noticed that a young, muscular workman with hair the color of a bursting sunrise was standing with his back to me. I watched him as he moved into a circle of men huddled around an open furnace. He lifted a long, slender tube from a rack around the furnace. On the end of the tube was a lump of tallowy substance about the size of a cantaloupe. It was shapeless and dull and, to my inexperienced eye, had nothing in common with the glistening crystal I had seen displayed in the shops. But that lackluster, formless, apparently useless object was to become a lovely piece of Steuben glass.

The workman rolled the tube carefully in his hands until the weight and motion caused a gradual change in the shapelessness of the melonlike object. Every few minutes, the slender tube was returned to the furnace rack, and the still formless object was thrust again into the furnace. The heat of the furnace made the object malleable for the shaping; as it became resistant, it was again thrust into the furnace. First, the furnace, then the shaping; then the furnace, then the shaping.

I began to wonder if any design would come to my chosen piece of embryonic glass. Then, almost imperceptibly, I saw the base swell into a gradual roundness, and from it came a necklike extension still attached to the tube in the worker's hand. It was to be a goblet!

It seemed as if the piece of glass sensed its design and responded more quickly to the processing. The times in the furnace were briefer, and I thought I saw greater care in the workman's timing of these periods. My gaze must have penetrated the windowpane and somehow nudged the workman's back because he turned to me, grinned, and lifted the tube in my direction. It was indeed a goblet. Dull and primitive in design, but surely a goblet. I clapped my hands. I thought it would soon be taken to the shelves of the showroom.

Although the workman appreciated my applause, I was wrong in my estimate of the goblet's progress. The work had scarcely begun. Other workmen took the goblet in their hands. There was more shaping. The neck developed a lip around the tube; the base became smooth and clearly fashioned. Infrequently, the action in the furnace was repeated. I thought, Hold on, little goblet. We're gonna make it!

Then an older man stepped into view. He lifted the tube and looked intently at the goblet, licking his lips as though he tasted the fineness of the work he was to do. He moved to the center of the room, and the activity around him lulled for a moment. Everyone watched as he raised the tube to his lips like a trumpet. In one moment of artistry, he blew a puff of air, a sigh from a master glass blower. A bubble was born in the neck of the goblet, a glistening dimple.

Again I clapped my hands, but the work still wasn't over. Taken from its umbilical tube, my goblet moved from station to station. It was polished, it was rubbed, it was fashioned. At the end of the assembly line sat a gray-haired woman under an extremely bright light. Her glasses had lenses so thick I could scarcely see her eyes. She picked up my goblet, held it up to the bright light above her, turned it between her hands, stroked its design with the fingers of her right hand, and finally squinted at one spot below the neck's bubble. Then she placed the newly produced goblet on a small bench beside her desk, picked up a wooden mallet and, with one quick gesture, smashed my goblet into jagged pieces!

The broken fragments were swept into a cardboard box beneath the bench. The wooden mallet was returned to the bench, and without so much as a shrug of concern, the woman turned her attention to the next object awaiting her approval.

I was stunned. My goblet! Broken and discarded, relegated to an untitled cardboard box instead of splendidly displayed on a showroom shelf. I must have cried out an involuntary "No!" for a gentleman wearing a blue jacket labeled "Guide" came to me.

"Why did she do that?" I asked. "That woman broke the goblet I've been watching since it began as a blob on a tube."

The guide turned to the station I was watching. "Yes, that's why she's there. She's our final inspector."

"But why did she do it?" I asked.

"It wasn't perfect," he answered. "Must have had some flaw."

"I was going to buy it!" I had purposely picked out one

that was small enough for me to afford. Some flaw? I wouldn't have minded. They could have marked it down. It could at least rate a "shelf of imperfects"—marked down 15 percent. "Why break it?" I asked.

"We always do that," he said. "She checks them before they go to the next stage."

"Another stage? Good heavens! That one goblet has been in and out of the furnace a dozen times. It's gone from craftsman to craftsman. What's next?" I asked the guide. I was personally involved with a goblet whose name I didn't even know.

"What happens at the next stage?" the blue-jacketed man replied. To answer, he led me to a small alcove where several workers were bent over a long table of crystal objects. "At the next stage, we inscribe the name of Steuben on the base. Once it has the name, it is perfect."

Process! We are beings in process. In and out of the furnace of experiences we encounter. Indwelt with the Master's breath, we are still polished and shaped and structured so that when we are fully mature—perfect— we might have the Master's signature. God is moving in us because we will carry His signature out into the world.

Remember, God's created being is considered valuable even before the process begins. See the care taken to lift the shapeless, unfashioned lump from the fire. See the attention given to each detail. Indwelt. Ennobled. Signed. Sealed. Oh, goblets in process, God loves you! You are extremely valuable to Him. Agree with His evaluation.

It took me a long time to realize that my nurtured, frequently misnamed inferiority complex was my telling God, "What You have called good, I will call worthless." I, under the guise of humility, would stand on my trembling tiptoes and call out to God that He was wrong in His estimation. Anytime we disagree with God, no matter how obsequious we seem to be, it is sin. What God has called good is good. What God has called valuable is valuable.

I would love to say that I'm no longer bothered by the dilemma of identity. But I want to be honest. In order to write this book, I had to deal with ghosts from that dilemma: creatures in the shadow of my good intentions, asking me what kind of person must I be to write a book people would actually buy—and even read!

The dilemma of identity needs a constant answer because the question is habitual: Who do you think you are to write a book or teach a class or take that job or marry that absolutely wonderful man waiting for you at the altar (who is wondering at this very moment, who does he think he is to marry someone as wonderful as you)? That persistent whisper of doubt limits God's handiwork in us like a not-yet-dry manicure makes a handshake awkward. There is a solution. God Himself moves to give the answer. Then we move to correct the habit. That takes time. Process. Again, process. But we are ill at ease in process until we claim that which substantiates process: *identity* or personhood.

Travel Tip:
Personhood is realized in process.

Identity is thought to be a lot of things it isn't, and identity isn't a lot of things it's thought to be. In order to understand identity, we must clear away the false definitions. For instance, we often think identity is a by-product of activity. When we want to know who someone is, we open conversations with "Tell me, what do you *do*?" What a person does is not who he is.

IDENTITY IS NOT A BY-PRODUCT OF ACTIVITY

I usually start my day with a two-mile walk with my husband, who usually starts his day figuring out how he can shorten that two-mile walk. During the day, I may fix breakfast and make sandwiches for my husband's lunch. I may conduct a staff meeting at our theater, sign payroll checks, plan a luncheon for a friend, grocery shop, go to an A.D. Players rehearsal, and then pack my bag for a trip to Wisconsin. I do all those things. They are tasks, but they do not make up who I am.

This is an important premise because our activities change. Rain cancels our walk, we run out of bread for sandwiches, staff positions are shuffled like aspen leaves in a fall wind. Friends move out of town, rehearsals are completed, grocery stores close, and bookings are canceled because the conferees decide they'd rather save their money for a well-known singer like Amy Grant. Activities change. The economy tumbles, and vice presidents of corporations become clerks. Even teenagers sometimes learn to make their beds, leaving an awkward space in the agenda of a parent whose identity is only in the parenting. Activities change and so do our relationships. Identity is not a by-product of activity or human relationships.

IDENTITY IS NOT A BY-PRODUCT OF RELATIONSHIPS

I once thought it was. When I went to New York City, I was very eager for that wonderful thing called "Success and Instant Stardom" to happen to me. I was in a little trouble, however, since I was scared to cross the street.

29

Whatever was going to happen to me had to happen on my corner.

I went to a bank on my corner, took my remaining traveler's checks and a little cash, and opened an account. The next week, I went to the bank to get some cash. The teller looked at my check, consulted her records, and came back to tell me she was very sorry but she wouldn't be able to cash my check.

"Why not?" I asked.

"Because you just opened an account, and it takes two weeks for an account to clear."

"But I *gave* you all my money . . ." I protested. Still she was adamant: two weeks for my account to clear.

I didn't know what to do. Somehow, I worked my way into the office of one of the vice presidents of Chase Manhattan Bank. Thick carpet. Awesome desk. Gracious gentleman standing there asking me what my problem was. I told him. And he told me it would take two weeks for my account to clear.

I looked him straight in the eye and with great certainty said to him, "I am Hubert E. Clift's daughter."

I'd grown up when Houston was a reasonably sized town, and everybody that I knew, knew my daddy. That day, standing ankle deep in carpet, I learned a mighty lesson: *Identity is not a by-product of human relationships.* If identity is secured by human relationships or by activity, it is doomed to the doubt of devastating changes.

True identity is a gift from God. He is constant. He says to you and to me, "I create whole beings. You will, in Me, be a whole person."

IDENTITY IS A GIFT FROM GOD

Few Scriptures speak so clearly of personal identity as those that tell about Moses' call from God in the third

30

chapter of Exodus. You remember the background. The people of Israel had lived in captivity in Egypt for over four hundred years. Moses figured that God had chosen him to lead Israel out of bondage, figured that Israel would recognize his godly appointment, and figured that God needed a little prodding as to the right time for action. So, he did a dumb thing that almost got him off God's course entirely. He killed an Egyptian, tried to paste his unorthodox authority over his fellow Jews, and ended up on the backside of the desert, tending sheep. Apparently, God thought tending sheep would be the best means for Moses to gain experience with people—like training nurses to give shots by letting them stab away at potatoes and oranges. Well, sitting out forty years on the backside of the desert, Moses began to wonder if he was going to gain anything other than a really super wife and several inauspicious sheepskins.

He was going home from work one day when he beheld a most wondrous sight—a bush aflame that wasn't consumed by its fire. Once Moses stopped to seek out the principle behind the performance, God knew Moses was ready for his magnificent assignment.

"Take off your sandals, Moses," God said. (The ground on which we offer our vulnerability to God's truth is in itself holy.) Then God assured Moses, "I have seen the oppression of My people who are in Egypt. I will send you to Pharaoh so you may bring the children of Israel out of Egypt."

"Oh, God," Moses said, digging his unsandaled toe in the sand. "I could never bring the sons of Israel out of Egypt! I couldn't ask them to follow me! Shoot! I've barely learned shepherding in forty years. I'm just not the man for the job. Besides, I didn't come here to apply. I just wondered why this bushy light didn't go out! And the people, God, they didn't follow me before, so they won't follow me now. Remember, God, I tried that tactic once, and it didn't work."

"Who am I," Moses asked, "that I should go to Pharaoh?"[1]

Note that Moses was sent into the backside of the desert to learn humility but learned a little more of it than was pleasing to God. A little self-deprecation may pass for modesty once in a while, but denying the right of God's appointment is nothing but pride wearing a fake halo. The refrain of feigned lowliness doesn't work for you or me. Don't worry about it; it didn't work for Jonah or Moses either.

Is there an opportunity or task facing you now? Something pleasing to God but surpassing your estimate of your ability? Do you mutter, "Who am I to do this? I'll never make it"? Identify with Moses and listen for God's answer.

God said, "I will be with you . . . for I have sent you." Identity is assured not by our action but by our reaction to God.

Moses continued his argument. "Okay, suppose I do as You say. And then they ask for Your name. What shall I answer?"

God said, "This is My name, I AM WHO I AM. Jehovah. Lord. The One who causes all things to be."

That, dear reader, that, Jeannette, *that* is the one and only source of true identity. Knowing His name means knowing His character, and in knowing Him, you will find your own validity in being His.

Paul taught the Corinthian Christians, "By the grace of God I am what I am," [2] and "If anyone is in Christ, he is a new creation."[3] Created fresh. Whole.

Let me tell you some great good news. God doesn't create fragments. He creates whole beings. The believer is one whose identity is secured by the One who never changes. By the grace of God, I am what I am. A person. Whole, under His authority. "To them He gave the *right to become* children of God, even to those who believe in His name."[4] I'm convinced that our struggle for identity can be met only in the One who causes all things to be.

Respect the authenticity of God's gift of personhood. Claim that identity and hold onto it with integrity. Identity will validate you throughout your travels.

Travel Tip:
Personhood is *practiced* in integrity.

I learned the importance of this travel tip when I was playing the part of Mrs. Malaprop in a wonderful production of *The Rivals* by Sheridan. The costumes were marvelous, and the set was a creative masterpiece. The design was such that the various set pieces would change positions during the play's progress, and in that way, scenes changed in full view of the audience.

During our technical rehearsal, the magic of such a theatrical wonderland became a tedious matter of detail. One large set piece, upstage left, had to move rapidly downstage center. But the piece didn't move rapidly, so the rehearsal stopped. The stage crew took their positions on the corners of the set piece and pushed and shoved with appropriate sounds and expressions. A slight tremor within the piece was the only response.

The director yelled at the stage manager, "I want that set piece to move quickly and quietly downstage center."

The stage manager hurried to enlist further crew members who managed to get the great hunk to move downstage slowly, like a dowager cruise ship puffing into harbor. The director had a silent, swift swan in mind. He demanded that additional crew members help to move the offending set piece "from upstage left to downstage center, like that!" The "like that" was accompanied by a pistol shot from the director's determined fingers.

Crew members were swarming all over the set. Casters were attached to the corners, adding a metal twirling to what should have been a silent move. The set piece creaked as it inched its way downstage.

The head carpenter was summoned and told, "I want that set piece to move from upstage left to downstage center, like that." Another snap of fingers. The head carpenter added rollers to complement the casters, and we had a full orchestra of tinkling, whirling sounds while ten crew members tried to look inconspicuous as they lugged the scenery along its directed path.

The director was now sitting in the audience looking a bit like Mount Saint Helens immediately prior to its explosion. Most directors were actors before they grew up. Under pressure, they frequently resort to the histrionics of their adolescence. Finally, the set designer was called.

Those of you who haven't been around theater may not fully understand what that means. Set designers are generally "underjoyed" when called by the director to correct something on the set, so a great tension always accompanies such a confrontation.

The director stood and said, "I want *that* set piece to move quickly from its upstage position to center stage, like that!" Loud finger snap.

Then silence. We actors were all watching, glad to be in the right place, glad it was the set piece doing the wrong thing.

The designer looked intently at the set piece. Then he walked all the way from far upstage very slowly down across the stage, right to the footlights. He leaned over the footlights and said to the director, "It cannot make that move. It would *go against the integrity of the piece.*"

The set designer's words cut through the makeup and the feathered hat and the layered fabrics of Mrs. Malaprop's outlandish costume. I heard them. I recognized the principle. The Bible gives us bywords of wisdom, which are thousands of years old but as relevant as our daily calendar: "The integrity of the upright will guide them."[5] We cannot go against the integrity of the piece! The authenticity of the being God has created must be respected.

Choices

Anyone with even the merest beginnings of maturity finds an array of choices frequently punctuating his daily agenda. Some are serious, some are trivial, but all require decisions. Unless we practice the tragedy of withdrawal, we must decide. What is the right thing to do? What is the most productive option to take?

If we are wise, we will get counsel from persons we respect. We will pray. We will go to the Bible. We will utilize our previous experience and take the necessary time to make a thoughtful decision.

Still, ultimately, we *must* choose. I often find that difficult. I don't like to make choices. I like to put off decisions until someone else has to make them, and then, no matter how it turns out, I can come out ahead. But one thing I'm learning is that God holds us accountable for our maturity—and mature adults must make choices.

Sometimes the options are in conflict. I see so many things I want to do. There are opportunities to speak to different conferences, which take time for preparation as well as long hours of travel. The growth of the A.D. Players demands my attention as writer, artistic director, coach, and enthusiastic participant. There are scripts offered me, which invite me into the commitment of acting, and friendships, which invite me into the commitment of sharing activities. Calls and causes that touch my heart plead for status on my agenda. So many things I want to do. Did you know that awareness of need doesn't constitute a call? Awareness of the need may only constitute *communication* of the need, not necessarily an *assignment* to the need. The choices must be considered.

Sometimes the choices are between what is godly good and what seems good but doesn't ring true. I've been in theater for many years. Theater frequently speaks a language and preaches a dictum out of sync with the tenets of my faith. Choices must be made. Will I play a certain role if its effect on the audience will be degrading rather than uplifting? I also have to think of my development as an artist. The artist speaks of life in its reality as he sees it.

"The integrity of the upright will guide them." My choices are to be directed by that principle. As a whole being, created by God, I must not go against the Designer's intention. If I do, I am threatening the integrity of my authenticity. The Designer knows this, so He remains a part of the process.

Jesus Christ prayed for a group of people who were not unlike us today. People lifted out of the ordinary by the fact of His choosing them: fishermen, a tax collector, a zealot, all humble men. Their faith was valid not because they were men of strength but because their faith rested in Jesus Christ. Christ prayed for that small collection of men through whom He would turn the world upside down. As He prayed for them, He prayed for us. Yes, He, Jesus Christ, prayed for you.

In the A.D. Players, we have a system of Prayer Shadows, people who commit themselves to daily prayer for the company member they shadow. Each of us knows that every day we have been specifically and effectively prayed for or shadowed by prayer. It's an incredible comfort. Each season as each one of us selects his or her prayer shadow, we choose carefully. We select people who know our circumstances and can therefore pray specifically for our needs. We select people who will keep in close communion with God and can therefore have access to Him on our behalf. We select mature Christians who will not take lightly the assignment of prayer.

Now, think of the One who shadowed us in the Garden of Gethsemane the night before His arrest, betrayal, and crucifixion. He knew what was ahead for Him. Every perfect muscle in that perfect body sensed the urgency of those few hours, and yet, He considered us worthy of His most intimate prayers! He was in perfect communion with God and in perfect identification with our circumstances. His prayer for us was perfect.

That night in Gethsemane, Jesus prayed for His disciples (and for us), "Father, keep these (my little bunch of disciples, my scant handful of followers in process). Keep them in Your name—those whom You have given me—that they may be one as We are One."[6] Keep them! They were very ordinary people. Subject to the same errors and failures as you and I. Those rank beginners had made bold statements of unfaltering faith that they wouldn't keep in the night of battle. They were so weary they fell into an exhausted sleep. They didn't look like much of an army as they slept sprawled on the ground. He cried out to God, "Keep them. They are valuable."

An incident in my life gave me a hint of Christ's viewpoint as He prayed for those He saw as valuable. One day a cat visited our house. My husband Lorraine and I said to each other, "Don't feed it. If you do, it will stay." Still, we fed the cat, and as we had suspected, it stayed. One morning the fat, happy cat thanked us by giving birth to five kittens. We found them in the garage, nestled in a crate of rusty coat hangers.

Daily, Lorraine and I would go out and move those kittens from that dangerous place to a more secure place, and the cat would move them back to the coat hangers. I thought, *Now what am I gonna do with all these kittens*? I put a little ad in the paper. No answer. Finally, one of the churches in the area had a fair, and I agreed to offer one of the kittens to anybody who won a particular game. The next day a little girl called and said, "I won a kitten. I'm gonna come by tomorrow and get my kitten."

Oh, I was so excited. I said, "Would you like five?"

Lorraine and I went out to the little box. We took the lid off the box and looked down. Five little kittens, stepping on each other, little tails straight up and little feet going in all different directions at once.

Lorraine said, "Let's find the one we're going to give the little girl."

"Okay."

"How about this one?" he asked.

"Oh, no," I cried, "not that one. That's the sweetest of the bunch. That one is all-white. It's marvelous to have an all-white kitten."

"Okay. Let's take this one."

"One of the gray ones? But we've only got two gray ones. They're wonderful. It's very hard to find gray kittens, and they're perfectly matched."

"Well, how about this one?"

"That's the one that's got the little black mustache, and we call him Charlie Chaplin," I said. "We can't give that one away!"

"Well, okay. We'll give her this one."

"Not that one! That one's mine."

We looked down at the box of scruffy little kittens, and I said to Lorraine, "They're all keepers."

That's the way we look to Jesus. Falling all over each other, crying out for attention, skulking in one corner because we yearn so much for love that we dare not ask for it. We are in a box called the world, cramped with the rusting coat hangers of unsatisfying finery. Jesus lifts the lid and looks down at us. He looks carefully at each one. He says, "Father, they're all keepers." Hear this fact: You unto the Lord Jesus Christ are *valuable*. You are a keeper, and He is the One who keeps you as His child. Allow the process of development. Risk its joy. It's worth celebrating early because process is secured by the love of God and directed by the integrity of your God-given personhood.

THREE

Avoid the Tourist Traps

*F*or several years, I've had the privilege of speaking at the Lowell Berry Schools of Evangelism, which are offered concurrently with the Billy Graham crusades. I've learned to love and enjoy these opportunities, but I'll never forget the first time I was involved in this program.

Dr. Kenneth Chafin, who was my pastor and will always be a cherished friend, suggested me for the faculty during his tenure as dean. Within the affirming friendliness of Dr. Chafin's manner, I was delighted to accept the invitation. Later, the delight spilled out through the split seams of my self-doubt. I would be speaking to pastors, church leaders, significant Christian laymen; I would be sharing the platform with major Christian personalities: Dr. Charles Allen, then the pastor of Houston's First Methodist Church and a widely read, as well as prolific, writer; Dr. Lewis Drummond, president of the Southern Baptist Seminary in Louisville; Dr. D. James Kennedy, the pastor of Coral Ridge Presbyterian Church, one of the fastest growing churches in America, and the organizer of Evangelism Explosion; and Millie Dienert, one of the most articulate women in Christian ministry, who had organized international prayer programs and was well known worldwide as a conference speaker.

I began to fret over my absence of title, scholarship, and experience. As for my credits, I had a drama degree from a secular university, was a Navigator dropout, and had a husband who found it healthier to prefer cafeteria cooking to eating at home. Checking the calendar, I figured I had a month to become a theologian, a famous writer, a well-beloved preacher, or a world-famous speaker. I checked off the possibilities one by one. Since my opportunity to speak to an audience outside the United States seemed limited to making a long-distance telephone call to a friend in Canada, the likelihood of my becoming a world-famous speaker was remote. I seriously doubted I could crowd a preacher's calling, curriculum, and congregation into one short month. The only book that included my writing was one treasured by my mother: a black composition book featuring "A Story by Jeannette Clift, aged 7 1/2. *The Story of a Old Man and How He Got His Christmas Gift.*"

The option left for me was theologian. I poured over the most scholarly commentaries I could find, looked up Greek words (though I could never pronounce them), listened earnestly to Dr. Chafin's sermons, took detailed notes from Major Ian Thomas, Chuck Swindoll, and Robert Schuller. By the time I arrived at the meeting, I had a British accent and a Dallas Theological Seminary viewpoint; I was going to explode with positives and hold my Bible spilling open like Billy Graham. I thought I was ready, but as I entered the crowded auditorium, I was desperately ill at ease.

Dr. Chafin met me at the back of the auditorium. The sight of his loping walk made me feel better. I wanted to curl up in the comfort of his outstretched hand. We sat together on the platform waiting for my time to speak. I was engrossed in my notes, trying to shorten the gap between me and the academics. I was stressed, strained, stretched, and strategically stupid!

Dr. Chafin is uniquely able to extend his few shortcomings to the shortcomings of others. In that loving identification, he spoke past my mirage to me. He touched my arm to distract me from my studies. "Now, Jeannette, I don't want you to turn theologian on me." I was so startled I froze in the middle of a Greek verb.

Three things generally reactivate my well-disciplined stammer: weariness, eagerness, and shock. I had a good dose of all three. A whispered stammer becomes a slush of sibilants. I hissed at him, "B-b-but these are p-p-p-p-reacherssss."

He smiled at me. "I didn't bring you here to be a preacher. I wanted these preachers to hear *you*."

As I thought about his words, I realized that I had fallen into one of the tourist traps of our journey through life: I was wearing a false nametag.

TOURIST TRAP 1:
A FALSE NAMETAG

Like a four-year-old opening a brightly wrapped gift, I jettisoned the British accent and the seminary viewpoint before we finished the opening prayer. By the end of the hymn, I was free of a falsely jubilant attitude, and during the special music, I confronted the fact that my Bible would never spill out over my hand because both were too small.

I heard the specifically personal introduction with relief. None of those other people could have fit Dr. Chafin's description. That afternoon I spoke from my heart,
although it nearly dislodged my nametag with its thump-
ing. But it was the right nametag! In the light of my cor-
rected identity, I saw the hundreds of men and women
crowded into that auditorium as people: people who
preach or teach or minister in various callings of God,
people who hurt and heal, people who live in the complexity of daily agenda, people who share the experience of frailty in the unfailing strength of the Lord. I knew
what to say to them because their experience was much
like mine. Their gracious response after I finished told me
I had made the right decision. In that affirmation, I added
a new travel tip to the margin of future itineraries.

Travel Tip:

Remove the old tatters of false nametags,
and wipe clean the label for your true identity.

The Bible makes it very clear that God never enjoins us
to wear another's nametag, carry another's assignment,
or assume another's calling. Instead, the Bible directs us
over and over again to the practice of our own unique
wholeness. When we don't know that wholeness, we become irritable, frustrated, angry, constantly threatened,
run down, wound up, and worn out. It is my personal
feeling that a lot of what is popularly called burnout is
caused by the excess weight of fake nametags. Believe
me, I know how unbearably heavy that load can be.

The Burden of Wearing a False Nametag

Soon after *The Hiding Place* became popular, I found myself in circles of higher cotton than I had ever chopped. I came back from the filming much like the person who had gone to the filming, but people perceived me differently. Thousands of people saw me not as Jeannette but as Corrie ten Boom. Because of Corrie's wisdom, I was expected to be wise. With very little warning, I found myself on platforms with Christian leaders far beyond my own understanding.

I was asked in public about controversial issues I had never known existed. Television interviews probed at the heart of experiences that had no reality in me. Like a drunken man trying to walk a straight line, I grabbed at anything for balance.

More mature Christians claimed pertinent joy from Bible verses I didn't understand. Instead of probing personally for their meaning, I copied the result. Moses sought the answer in the burning bush; I sought to mimic the flames. When questioned for spiritual truths, I quick-coded the stock of ready answers and handed out responses like a bakery dispenses numbers to shoppers waiting their turns. I spoke of unfaltering joy while my own heart fluttered in its faltering. Not knowing has never kept me from answering; it only turns up my volume. This wasn't a case of my expecting too much of myself. This was a case of others expecting me to be somebody else. I loved Corrie. I loved *The Hiding Place*. I believed in its ministry, rejoiced in its excellence, and wanted very much to serve any aspect of that film's assignment.

No one forced me to take this fake nametag. No one associated with the film asked me to go along with this posture. Certainly, Corrie never asked it of me. Her only stated displeasure with me was that I wore pants suits and spoke in a Texas accent her ears couldn't fathom. She offered me unconditional love, and in her presence, I was welcome. Her secretary-companion, Ellen, became a friendly bulwark in the swirling soirees of Christian popularity. Jim Collier, the director of *The Hiding Place*, and his wife Emmy were true and genuine friends, as were the staff and production geniuses of the filming. Tedd Smith, whose hands and mind bring forth music beyond compare, opened those hands to me in a blessing of friendship. I don't think anyone I knew ever did a number on me, but I did one on myself.

I switched my nametag and fell into the common tourist trap of trying to be someone I wasn't! I learned a great unalterable truth. When my public profession outdistances my private confession, I fall into the gap in between.

As I write this book, I must deal with those fading reminders of error and proven inadequacy. I ask myself, *Can you, the reader, accept me, the writer, as I truly am? Is this book to be yet another paste-up Jeannette?*

God has limited the options. It was a gracious thing to do. I am me and can write only as me. I am a woman facing middle age who has made many mistakes, but I am also a woman occupied by God who has—in *me*—done many things right.

It isn't always easy to drop a false nametag because negatives can hinder that positive action. Let's look at how that can happen.

1. We Like the False Nametag. We may feel a false nametag has served us well; therefore, we consider it standard equipment. However, any travel group we crash while hiding behind a false nametag will dampen our party spirit with the responsibility of constant pretense.

Any relationship based on deceit must be maintained by deceit. Sooner or later, we want out of it because deceit is a tyrannical taskmaster.

In *Gone With the Wind*, Prissy places herself in a role of trustworthiness by assuring Miss Scarlett she knows all about "birffing babies," but when confronted by Miss Melly's time of birthing, Prissy wants out of the trustworthy role—and in a hurry. There is rich laughter as Butterfly McQueen portrays Prissy's difficulty, but when we deal with the tragedy of false nametags, the audience seldom laughs.

2. We Fear the Response. When we discard that false nametag, we have to consider our immediate society, which may have been more at ease with the fake than the real. We have to learn to sympathize with their loss as we celebrate our gain. We also need to be sure that the choices we make are in keeping with the authority of God and not the petulance of self-will.

I can't flaunt my identity and hurt the people around me. For instance, one trivial example of this comes to mind from a theater experience. A friend of mine, Maggie O'Brien, is an exceptionally fine actress, and one season she was playing a leading role in an off-Broadway show. In the closing act, she had a major speech. One night, the actor playing the scene with her began to interpolate small distracting actions into her scene. He pulled at her arm is if to interrupt her. Maggie brushed him off and continued. The next night, the actor added ad-lib mutterings that interfered with the structure of the scene. Each night, this pattern of interference was handled without departing from the play. (Maggie is a gracious lady, and she was able to maintain her character without stopping the play's progress.) But one night as Maggie was saying her lines, the actor grabbed her and clamped his hand over her mouth! They struggled for a few seconds until Maggie freed herself and finished the scene.

Afterward, Maggie followed the disciplinary process of theater and reported the incident to the stage manager, who rebuked the actor. Maggie, still sputtering at the outrage done her performance, looked up to see the actor standing in the doorway of her dressing room. He said, "I don't know why it upsets you so much. It *worked for me!*" It worked for him to the detriment of the scene, to the discomfort of his fellow performer, and to the denial of proper authority.

A trick like this is a misuse of my freedom to be who I am. Self-will shouldn't be confused with my God-given identity. In time, we learn to keep our mouths shut and our minds open, instead of rashly reversing the process. We learn to trust God, whose flexible love never dims His identity.

The Joy of Being Who You Are

An incident in my life clarified for me the value of true nametags. About six years ago, I was speaking at a luncheon held in the civic auditorium of a city in Oklahoma. It was obvious that great care had been taken in the planning for this event, for about four hundred well-dressed ladies were seated at tables made festive by tablecloths improvised from pink-bordered bedsheets. I settled myself at my place at the head table and heard the luncheon chairwoman announce that the centerpieces and tablecloths were for sale. A small murmur echoed her words as the ladies discussed which centerpieces and cloth would be purchased by which lady.

I picked up my fork and noticed that two rose-petaled radishes adorned my salad. Someone had taken the time to pretty up two radishes, just for me. Then I noticed that

each salad at the head table had two neatly curled radishes. I knew the group hosting the luncheon had prepared the meal and was impressed that an extra touch
had been added for the table of honored guests. I turned
to the lady sitting to my right, who was at that moment
looking over her notes for the introductions.

"I'm impressed by the radishes," I said.

She looked at her notes to see if this quirk of impression was referred to in my biography. It wasn't.

"You're impressed by what?" she asked.

"The radishes," I said. "Look, each salad plate at our
table has curled radishes."

"Yes," she said, exercising a smile that must have been
standard for dealing with unorthodox speakers. "They're
pretty."

"They're more than pretty," I said. "Someone took special care to do these."

"Don't they all have them?" she asked, gazing out at
the tables.

I looked and was astonished. As far as I could see,
each salad plate was adorned with two curled radishes,
posing in the fringe of lettuce leaves.

My table partner abandoned her list to glean fresh
information from the actual subject. "Do you like radishes?" she asked.

"Yes, but that's not what's important. They are curled.
That's hundreds of radishes! That took a lot of time!"

The lady to my right seemed a bit bewildered by my
enthusiasm for radishes, so I explained, "I only do curled
radishes for special occasions—and never for more than
just a few people. It's an extra nicety and I appreciate it."

"I'm not on the planning committee, but Gertrude is.
I've been working with program personnel." She turned
to get the attention of Gertrude, three chairs down, who
was at that time earnestly assuring the soprano soloist

that her accompanist would surely be present in a matter of minutes.

"Don't bother her," I said. "I can tell her later."

"It's no bother," Miss Program Personnel whispered and leaned over the lady-who-designed-the-center-pieces and the lady-in-charge-of-the-nursery to call to Gertrude, the lady-in-charge-of-planning. "Mrs. George wants to ask you something about the radishes."

"The what?" Miss Planning mouthed back.

"The RA-DI-SHES!"

The lady-in-charge-of-designing-the-centerpieces, thinking I was saying something about her work, smiled at me as her tongue dislodged a bit of parsley from her front teeth. The other lady, the lady-in-charge-of-the-nursery, looked at her radishes one by one. I no longer cared. I sat with my head bowed, hoping people would think I was too deep in prayer to be involved in the radish brouhaha! I felt a tap on my shoulder, turned around, and there, kneeling beside me, was Gertrude.

"Is there something wrong with your radishes?" she asked.

"No. They are fine. I just thought it was nice to have them all curled."

"Oh, Marietta does those."

"All of them?"

"Yes, she says that's her contribution. She and her children did them yesterday, and she brought them early this morning in a freezer chest."

I knew the headcount in the room and was astonished. "That's almost eight hundred radishes!"

"Yes, but Marietta wants to do it. Would you like to meet her? She's in the kitchen."

So Gertrude and I went into the kitchen, and there I met Marietta, the lady-of-the-radishes, who was wearing a pink print apron over a dark green cotton dress with a

49

white Peter Pan collar that had "Kitty" embroidered on
it. She was sitting at a round table with other ladies who
had served the lunch. Her gray hair was short and looked
like a tight wool cap. As we walked toward her, all the
ladies joined in greeting Gertrude, while Marietta smiled
at us, obviously wondering why our attention was directed to her. We were introduced amid the frittering of
ladies offering me biscuits or coffee.

"Is your nickname Kitty?" I asked.

"No."

"I noticed the name on your collar."

"Oh, this is my daughter's dress. I borrowed it . . . for
the party."

"Gertrude tells me you curled all those radishes.
They're lovely. Each salad looks so . . . festive."

"I didn't mind doing it. It just takes time."

I didn't know what more to say, so I left, after thanking
the other ladies for their work for the luncheon. Gertrude
and I went back to the table and finished our meal. An-
nouncements were made; the singer sang. Someone won
a hand-crocheted telephone book cover for having the
most postage stamps in her purse. Another lady won a
centerpiece for driving the farthest to come to the meeting. I spoke, and there was encouraging response. Afterward, ladies scurried past me with murmured greetings,
and a few lingered to speak of God in their lives.

Tables were already being cleared, money for the centerpieces was being counted, when my hostess borrowed an umbrella. It was raining heavily, so we hurried
across the parking area to the car. Through the rain, I
could see a lady, carrying a large red-and-green polka-
dot umbrella that had collapsed on one side, waiting by
our car. A small misty waterfall was tumbling from the
bright dots onto the small figure. It was Marietta! She was

smiling as though we had found her on a sunny day in an especially delightful garden.

"Marietta," I called to her, "what are you doing here? You're getting soaked."

She ignored my banal proclamation of the obvious and said, "I had to see you. I heard your speech. It was good."

My hostess was hastily unlocking the car door. I interrupted Marietta.

"Get inside. We can talk on the way to the airport."

"Oh, no," she said. "I have to go on home."

I slipped inside the car. Marietta crouched down close to the window, holding the working part of her umbrella over her head, and called to me, "Just remember this. You keep telling people about Jesus, and I'll keep curling the radishes."

The rain and my tears splattered the picture of her face as we started the car and backed out of the driveway. Nothing of that moment has faded in my memory. She and I waved to each other so long as we were joined in view. And, dear Marietta, I haven't forgotten. We are to do our two jobs in the love of Him who does all things well. Between the lady who makes the speeches and the lady who makes the radishes, there is no dilemma of false nametags . . . only the delight of fellowship.

TOURIST TRAP 2:
FAULTY CONNECTIONS

In 1985, I was scheduled to perform at the Buffalo Christian Center in Buffalo, New York. Kurt Kaiser, George Beverly Shea, and I were to present an evening of music and drama, and I looked forward to being with those two gifted artists as well as my friends, the Alan Forbeses.

My ticket looked like this:

	Flight	Date	Time
Houston Intercontinental			
Airport	1188	11/11/85	11:30 A.M.
Cleveland, Ohio			2:33 P.M.
Cleveland,			
Ohio	1616	11/11/85	3:01 P.M.
Buffalo, New York			4:40 P.M.

That afternoon the weather in Houston was bad, and my flight had a delayed departure. I checked with the agent at the boarding gate, and he assured me all the flight connections would be met. Since I was to fly to Cleveland for my flight to Buffalo, I was primarily concerned about my luggage being transferred during what was a scant few minutes between planes.

As I boarded, I asked the flight attendant to check my connections in Cleveland, and she said, without looking at my ticket, "Oh, don't worry. We'll make up the time." Thus assured, I settled back to worry about the ordinary concerns of flying—every bump, twist, and rocking motion of the plane.

The weather was dreadful, the flight so bumpy that the attendants began to look as ashen as the passengers. I always read the condition of the attendants as a barometer for the condition of the flight and usually shift into high terror when those efficient people are directed to "stay seated until we pass through this turbulence." This time, I was more concerned about my plane out of Cleveland than the turbulence into Cleveland.

We began to circle the city as we threaded our way through the rough wool of storm clouds. I had my ticket sent to the pilot to be sure my flight to Buffalo would wait for me. I think it was the young stewardess's first day, and she had just decided to apply for a job in the alterations department of a well-grounded fashion shop, as she came swaying back toward me. She recited her lines with such precision I knew she was saying exactly what the pilot had said. "Yours is an illegal connection, and therefore, we do not have to honor it!"

I lead a fairly conservative life. I don't try to get eleven items through the quick check lane at the grocery store. I always clean out the airplane lavatory "for the next passenger's use." I never remove the little tags on new pillows that say "DO NOT REMOVE," and I was once reprimanded by a policeman for holding up traffic on the freeway by obeying the speed limit! To me, the term *illegal* has fervent meaning and is seldom, if ever, applied to my actions.

"Why is this connection illegal?" I whispered.

"It's less than thirty minutes" was the newly memorized answer.

"But it's on my ticket, and it's printed in your timetable," I said, holding up the little booklet I had been studying, trying to find another flight to Buffalo that would meet my performance schedule.

This was new information. It didn't compute with what had just been memorized, so she scurried back to the judicial chambers of the pilot. Well, the higher courts of that airline decided that they would do their best to facilitate my connection and moved me to a front seat so I might make a hasty transfer.

As soon as we landed, the attendant said, "Come on,

Mrs. George. I'll lead you to our ground supervisor who will take you to your plane."

We ran from the still-wheezing airplane onto the jetway. Once we reached an ascending hallway, my energetic escort left me. Another uniformed attendant, smiling and waving a torn computer print-out, stood at the top of the hallway. "Mrs. George?" he called.

"Yes," I yelled back, struggling with all my hand luggage as I ran up the ramp.

"Hurry, Mrs. George. I'm here to help you."

I nearly fell into his arms as I cleared the gate. *You could have helped me by offering to carry either one of my bulky carry-ons, leaving me to manage only my purse, typewriter, and copy of* USA TODAY, I thought.

He again asked, "Mrs. George?"

I nodded.

"Well, you missed your plane! It left about ten minutes ago. It was full."

I was staggered by more than my carry-ons, purse, typewriter, and USA *Today*. "Full? It couldn't have been full. I was supposed to be on it!"

"Those things happen," he said, merrily reading the details of the next plane to Buffalo, which would get me to the theater approximately two hours and twenty minutes after my program. "We're sorry about this." His tone held no hint of sorrow, so I assumed the "we" referred to the concert managers in Buffalo. Slightly withered by my aggressively accusing gaze, the young man lowered his voice, relinquished his smile, and spoke from under the near side of his mustache, "After all, Mrs. George, yours is an *illegal connection!*"

Again I added a travel tip to the margins of my journey through life.

Travel Tip:
Check the connections. Make sure they work
in the reality of every day.

My connections between Cleveland and Buffalo might
have worked in a smaller town, but not in a city airport
like the one in Cleveland. And not during stormy weather.
Those connections didn't coincide with the reality of that
day in Cleveland.

Faulty connections don't just happen only on air
flights. Life's filled with them. Let me tell you of two faulty
connections between fact and fiction that almost scut-
tled my marriage.

When Lorraine asked me to marry him about fifteen
years ago, I professed great disinterest in any of the tra-
ditional wedding accouterments. I wanted no engagement ring, no wedding attendant, no wedding dress, no
reception. Those were for eighteen-year-olds. A private
ceremony would be best for two adults.

Three weeks before the wedding, I suddenly burst into
tears as Lorraine and I were driving back from a weekly
Bible class. Whimpering like an underfed cat, I moaned,
"I don't have anything that says I'm engaged!"

Lorraine had offered me an engagement ring, which I
had refused with the ornate disdain of assumed practi-
cality. Now, bewildered by my tears, he began to address
the verbal deciphering that would be practiced frequently in the years ahead.

"What kind of 'thing' do you want that would say
you're engaged?"

"I don't know," I sniffled, "but something I could have
all the time."

"You mean something like a letter?"

"No, Lorraine! *Not a letter!*"

"Do you mean something you could carry with you?"

"Not exactly . . ."

"Something you could hold in your hand?"

"That might help."

"Something you could wear?"

"That sounds like a good idea."

"Like a ring?"

I heard it as though for the first time. I wasn't pretending. Suddenly, tradition had touched my life and become reasonable. I was given my lovely pearl engagement ring in the chapel of St. John the Divine's Episcopal Church in Houston, Texas, and love, pledged in private, became official as it rested auspiciously on my left hand.

In the next week, the wedding plans also changed. I asked Dolores Tidwell, a friend since junior high school days, to be my wedding attendant. My mother called Dolores her "other daughter," and in that friendship, the tradition of loyalty touched my life and became trustworthy. My friend Jody Elliott, who was to sing at the wedding, sang possible selections to me from department store dressing rooms while I tried on wedding dresses. The one I chose was beautiful, and the pictures of our wedding reception are cherished mementos of a happy occasion.

All the traditions made joyous contact with our lives. Well, almost all. As a child, I had always dreamed of having my favorite hymn, "Amazing Grace," sung at my wedding. However, I only married fifteen years ago, and the thought of my marching down the aisle at that age while they sang "Amazing Grace" didn't fit well. Instead, we sang "The Church's One Foundation." Good, solid, substantial statement.

But I still hadn't learned how to avoid faulty connections. I almost ruined my marriage in the first few weeks because I was confusing fiction with fact.

One night, soon after we returned from our honeymoon, Lorraine got home from work, and I met him at the elevator to our apartment with a glass of tomato juice.

I said, "Here, drink this because dinner's ready."

And he said, "Well, what kind of day did you have?"

And I said, "We don't have time to talk now."

He came in, and I served an elaborate salad on our new china salad plates. He obediently ate his salad, and I brought out a great platter of a wonderful fish dish. I put it on the table as I smiled to myself thinking about how nice everything looked: candles, flowers, shining monogrammed napkin rings. Then I looked at my watch. "Oh, dear, I'm going to have to leave to go to rehearsal."

Lorraine said he wanted to watch the rehearsal, so we left hurriedly. We came home late that night and learned an interesting thing: Fish that has been left in the center of the table for several hours can be smelled from the downstairs lobby before you ever get into the elevator.

The next night, I decided to be quicker. I met him downstairs with the tomato juice so he could drink it in the elevator going up. I served soup instead of salad. I thought it'd go down quicker. I came out with a platter filled with a wonderful chicken dish broiled with tangerines and artichokes, put it in the center of the table, looked at my watch, and said, "I've got to go to rehearsal."

"I want to watch that rehearsal, too," he said, as he had the night before.

So we left. Late that night, I learned chicken that has been sitting in the middle of the table smells just as bad as fish!

This went on for three nights. Late the third night, I

began crying as I scraped the food down the disposal. "I'll never get this right. I'll never be a good wife. We'll be broke because of food I've wasted."

Lorraine asked what every man should know not to ask, "What's the matter?" It is prescribed by law that we as wives answer, "Nothing!" If we *knew* what was the matter, we wouldn't be crying. Then Lorraine looked at me and said, "Honey, do you really want to eat all that food?"

"No."

"Neither do I. Why are we having it?"

"Because I saw it in a magazine," I admitted.

Illegal connections: The reality of my marriage didn't make contact with the fiction of a magazine picture. I wasn't allowing God to do the wonderful thing of creating a union that was new and of us.

Don't hinder God's plan in your life by the error of bad connections. Connect reality to reality. If it's necessary to my marriage to have a five-course meal every evening, I'll have to give up being at the theater by seven—or Lorraine will have to give up working (which is somewhat essential to our marriage). If it's part of our marriage for Lorraine to keep his job and for me to stay with the theater, I've got to abandon the picture of a five-course meal.

Not *all* marriages fit into the pattern of domestic structure that is successful for *most* marriages. Realistic orderliness, which is absolutely essential to our lives, must come from the realistic integrity of the people involved. Certain principles are simplistic in their application. If you don't want your husband to work with women, don't marry an obstetrician. If you want a job that fits comfortably into a nine-to-five time slot, don't go into theater. God's calling doesn't confuse this issue. If one has answered a call to serve in Bangladesh but one doesn't choose to leave Fort Wayne, Indiana, one must wait until

God directs the incorporation of Bangladesh into beautiful mid-America. I have seen and been part of the confused and frustrated Christian community trying to reconcile the unreconcilable. Fantasy and reality may enjoy an enchanting wedding, but they can have only a miserable marriage.

The A.D. Players confront this mystery with each level of our growth. You can't cram the wonder of what God is doing through Christian theater into the patterns already set for Christians and for theater. Several years ago, a church wanted me to establish a drama ministry for them. As we talked of their hopes and options, I became so excited that my dreams outdistanced theirs. They were planning to build a theater for our work, with an unlimited number of people eager to begin. They wanted to start with a major production that meant the plan was a serious endeavor aiming at continuity. I asked how long I would have for rehearsals and was astonished to hear that I would be given a five-week period. That is longer than the A.D. Players had to prepare for their performances!

It all seemed wonderful until I inquired about the time for the rehearsal. Only one time slot was available: from 5:45 to 6:45 each Sunday evening! My heart sank. Five rehearsals without continuity. It can't be done! The process would be aborted. By the time I left the meeting, I had redirected their interest to a series of short sketches, but I doubted that they understood. The dream was good. The structured hour was good. But the connection was faulty. We were trying to connect two ideas whose needs didn't match. Faulty connections.

Christ spoke of this principle as He taught the greater principle of the new life occupied by the Spirit of God. He said, "Put new wine into new wineskins."[1] New wine added to old wineskins makes up faulty connections that just won't work. That is why God comes to dwell in a life made new, and the life made new is suitable only for Him.

Have you learned the hard way the lesson of the Pharisees that fresh paint will not sweeten rotting sepulchers? If you have, look out for this tourist trap. Grab your suitcase, and check for any lingering fragments of faulty connections and false nametags. Your journey will be a lot smoother if you avoid these tourist traps.

FOUR

Trust Your Guide

*F*or most of my adult life, I've been in the entertainment business. As an actress, I've worked in theaters in Texas, New York, Washington, D.C., Pennsylvania, New Hampshire, Connecticut, and Maryland. Wherever I've performed, I've known and thanked God for the opportunity to practice the disciplined craft of artistic communication. Theater is an honorable medium that began in worship and is bursting with potential for godly communication.

However, I'm aware that the most popular voices of entertainment frequently speak nothing but hopelessness. A shocking reversal of the vital word of hope! Often the encouragement suggested in a play is nothing but a degrading adjustment to despair. We who receive that message are bombarded by despair. And we have accepted it as though there were no other rational alternative.

A glorious, rational alternative does exist. God *promises*

us hope. In Him, *hope* is the most reasonable word in the world. Jeremiah said to the sinning people of Judah, "'For I know the plans that I have for you,' declares the Lord, 'plans for welfare and not calamity . . . that you [put your name in here] _____ may have a future and a hope.'"[1] God says to us in the midst of our flight, in the midst of the process, in the midst of the circumstances of our lives, "I know My plans for you, and they are good!"

Note the intimacy of this verse. God said this to a people who had chosen to reject His laws and had placed themselves under the persuasion of pagan religions. These people, whom God had delivered, directed, nurtured, and loved, not only forsook Him but "walked after emptiness and became empty."

In reading the details of that period in Israel's history, we learn that sin had become a way of life, acceptable to all except God and the godly. In the name of tolerance, rulers, prophets, and priests had encouraged the blending of idolatry with the worship of the one true God. The uniqueness of Jehovah God had been forgotten. God in His absolute justice had no option but to administer discipline—punishment wrapped in the tears of a grieving Jeremiah who was to see the mighty city of Jerusalem fall because its citizens ignored his pleading for a return to God.

I have a print of Rembrandt's magnificent depiction of Jeremiah weeping over the ruins of Jerusalem. I study it often for what it tells me about this "prophet of doom." I see the body slumped into itself, one hand wearily supporting a head shuddering with grief. In the distance are the black thread figures of people who would not obey and now experience the reality of ruin.

And yet, to these people, God Himself held out hope. God, still loving, said, "I know My plans for you, and they are good." Even under discipline there is hope. In fact,

God, whose economy is perfect, does not waste His discipline; His purpose for discipline is to make those "good plans" possible. (We will address that assurance in chapter 6.)

Hope is the unique signature of the Christian gospel. Twenty years ago, I began a theater company to communicate that message of hope. We called ourselves the After Dinner Players because we hoped someone would get the hint and feed us before the show. Now we've grown to a twenty-two member, full-time company with a 208-seat theater in Houston, Texas, and a traveling itinerary throughout this country and Europe performing for conferences, churches, schools, theaters, and military bases. It's a great work, but it hasn't been easy. Twenty years is not a flicker of scene change; it has been and continues to be a process, a discipline, a unique pilgrimage. Somewhere along the way, we became the A.D. Players, and all along the way, we remind ourselves of the relevance of hope as well as the message of hope.

Many times quitting was the easiest thing to do once the challenge lost its glamour in the tedium of endurance. I remember one awesome evening in those early years of struggle. (Don't be confused; the "struggle" wasn't unique to those early years. We still struggle, but the years are no longer early.) We had rented a theater for a special performance since we had no property of our own. The tickets were all sold, a full house was expected, and we were readying the stage area for our performance.

I noticed a deep red stain on the stage and directed the crews to paint over it. They obeyed, but the red stain didn't. Finally, we realized that it came from the ceiling. An overloaded air-conditioning tower was leaking through the roof. Droplets of rusty water were spattering the stage and the first few rows of audience seats. We had a dilemma. We also had an audience arriving in four hours.

I called the theater owner to report the leak and was told he was so sorry about it but he could do nothing! I appreciated the sympathy, but it didn't solve our dilemma. We sent out a call for buckets to catch the smelly spatterings. We considered canceling the show but felt it was too late to locate the audience members. Again, I called the theater owner. He said we might find some solution in turning off the air conditioning. If it didn't rain, the spattering would lessen.

Turn off the air conditioning in September in Houston, Texas? Still, we turned off the air conditioning. We sweltered! Then it began to rain! It was 7:30 P.M. The audience would arrive in thirty minutes!

We gathered back in the dressing room to fret, to cry, and to pray. Unfortunately, in that order. The rain had stopped, but it was unbearably hot. The pattern of rusty puddles traced designs of despair on the stage. The buckets in the audience provided a discordant symphony of hopelessness. *Bing. Bong. Bing. Bong. . . .*

It always amazes me to find that faith is often the believer's last ditch stand. We prayed. I remember my prayer because it came from the twisted knots within my stomach and expressed an intention born in defeat. "Lord, we are a theater proclaiming hope. This is a good time for us to practice what we proclaim. You handled the matter of Noah's flood; You are bound to be able to take care of one air conditioner's overflow. If You want us to play through this experience with red water dripping on us and the audience, we will praise Your name in it. If that isn't consequential to Your plan, we would greatly appreciate it if You would cause the drippings to stop dripping. Thank You for this venture. Amen."

I sent two crew members out to paint away the last spill

stains and turn on the air conditioner. The cast was directed to stay in their dressing rooms and pray until they were ready to play in whatever circumstances God provided. I went out to greet the audience, sharing our dilemma with only two trusted friends who promised to pray with me as the show began. We waited a few minutes for the paint to dry, emptied the buckets, and did our play.

Not one drop of water fell on the stage or the audience!

My praying friends still think I was joking about the dilemma. The next morning the theater owner called me to return the rent money. I told him we played the program with no problem. He was stunned. He had canceled classes scheduled for the stage that morning because he knew the area would be awash with rusty spillings. As an extra touch from God, one of our cast members turned her life over to Christ, the Lord of crisis, during her performance that night.

Is rusty red water still dripping on your parade? Let me be very clear. Our miracle from God was realized before we ever left the dressing room. Sometimes His plan dries up the spillings, and sometimes His plan includes the spillings. The miracle is God's plan. We only have to retain hope in the midst of the plan. Too often our question is, Can we trust that plan *in* flight? Over the years, I've learned to trust God. I've found that we can't have hope without trust. Here are seven travel tips to remember as you try to trust God in the midst of your dilemmas.

Travel Tip 1:
You can trust God's plan for your life because *Jesus Christ became man.*

The person of Christ validates our hope. He Himself brings God and His infinite trustworthiness into view. In the opening verses of the incredible gospel of John, the apostle tells us about the unique character of the Word: pre-existent, self-creating, capable of fellowship. Then we read that the very Word who created everything gave Himself to creation and became flesh! We can't fully understand the miracle of John 1:14—"And the Word became flesh and dwelt among us"—but the miracle is the foundation for our hope.

Each Christmas I prop up a little card on the table in my hallway, right inside the door so everyone who enters our home is reminded of the joy of its message. It was given me by a very dear friend, Natalie Goodman, after she and I explored together the wonder of John 1:14. My little Holly Halo's bright red print letters say, "The wonder of Christmas is that God became man." I celebrate that thought each day of the year, but at Christmas, I can celebrate it louder because the whole world joins in the celebration. God so loved the world that He gave His only begotten Son! I never heard of any other god who moved toward me first. His plan can be trusted because He kept His promise, displayed His love, and personally explored my circumstances.

Travel Tip 2:
You can trust God's plan for your life because *Jesus Christ is the Good Shepherd.*

Jesus never called Himself the "Shepherd." He called Himself the "Good Shepherd." That means a lot to me. I'm an actress who has worked under many directors. Of all those directors, I would pick out only three or four I would call "good directors." When I think about those few, I realize that they didn't always choose to direct me in the way I chose to be directed. But each of those "good directors" led me to a good performance whether I agreed with him or not. Jesus is the Good Shepherd. We can trust Him to get His sheep home.

We all cuddle up to the phrases where Jesus calls us His sheep. We wrap ourselves in sentiment and smile tenderly at each other whispering, "We're His sheep." I wonder if we've missed the point. Have you ever really considered sheep?

I grew up in West Texas ranch country, and I saw a lot of sheep. None wore pink ribbon bows. And you knew they were there before you got to them. Nobody will ever try to bottle "Odour de Sheep."

Sheep will starve to death because they're not looking directly at the food. Sheep will die of dehydration because they're facing away from the water. One sheep will come to the edge of a cliff and fall off, and the others think, *That looks like fun*! Off they go, too, a whole bunch of them. Jesus wasn't giving us a compliment. I think He was saying, "You're sheep. You're in desperate need of a shepherd."

It's so encouraging to know that the Lord has never been tricked by the sheep. We may have been able to fool everybody else in the world but not Him. We may be under discipline, we may be in times of great suffering, we may know rough places and dry places, but He is the Good Shepherd. He'll get His sheep home! Not only is His direction trustworthy, but we can trust God because He is always near.

Travel Tip 3:
You can trust God's plan for your life because He is *holding you in the palm of His hand*.

God has said, ''I have inscribed you on the palm of My hand.''[2] Every once in a while, I ask myself, *What does it mean to be in the hand of God?*

Think about this with me. Look at your hand, just for a moment. Imagine that God's hand is like your hand, and see yourself in His hand. Follow the route. You may be in the middle, secure and settled in. Or you may have wandered over to the little finger. Or you might even have wandered out to the tip of the fingernail. (Have you ever felt God just sort of bouncing you back into the center again?)

If we are in the hand of God, we may make a lot of choices. We might choose the thumb. We might choose to travel around the outline. But if we're in the hand of God, we will go where the hand goes. He's got strong hands with a strong grip.

Some time ago, I was driving into Seattle with friends. I looked far ahead of us, and I saw a young man on a motorcycle. A young boy, apparently his son, was perched behind him. I thought, *Isn't that amazing? I wonder what's holding that little boy on the motorcycle? Maybe there is a brace.*

I got closer to him, and I looked again. No brace. *Maybe he's tied to his father.*

We got up closer to them, and I couldn't find a harness or a brace. (However, I must say that right behind them was a car driven by what looked very much like the mother, intently watching the two on the motorcycle.)

As we came up beside the cycle, I leaned my head out the window to see more clearly. Nothing was holding that little boy onto the security of his father except his little hands, gripping his father's leather jacket! That's dangerous! That's very dangerous! The trip was long. Little fingers get tired. And it was cold. Little fingers get stiff. And leather gets slippery. What kind of father would trust his son's safety to a child's grip on papa's leather jacket?

One of the reasons we're often frightened is that we think our God is that kind of father. I once thought I was held by my grip on Him. Since I knew I couldn't trust my grasp, I was unable to trust God. Praise the Lord and Hallelujah! We're *not* held by our grip on Him! We're held by His grip on us.

The tenacity of God's grip is assured by the character of God, which is revealed in many Scripture passages. One of particular relevance is in the book of Joshua. Joshua was a young soldier who had proven his mettle in battle and his faith in trusting God. He was faced with an awesome assignment; he was to take over the leadership of Israel after the death of Moses. Can you imagine what doubts and fears might have found their home in his heart? Have you ever been a replacement for a leader like Moses? Have you ever had to fill a hero's shoes with your own bunions and twisted little toe? Have you ever felt the mantle of leadership knotting its tassels around your throat?

I've been a replacement many times. Once in New York City, I went on for a leading lady after only one hurried rehearsal with the cast. That night before the show, I was at my dressing table, sturdy with the starch of terror. I kept staring into my own eyes in the mirrored reflection so I wouldn't have to see the concerned glances from the veterans of the cast. Theater people are by nature encouraging to their own and sympathetic to the performer under stress.

There is a haunting fragility about the ease of an actor's craft; each actor is like a lion tamer at the height of his proficiency who knows that the lions are really not tamed but only well conducted. All actors know that fragility and, even with the threat of personal loss, reach like worried young mothers to a fellow performer in need. One actor came over and hugged me saying, "Don't worry; you're going to be great." His hands on my shoulder were clammy, and his voice shook. I decided it was wiser to worry for both of us! The director trotted into the room and flashed a smile of extravagant confidence before crouching behind me and rattling off frantic last-minute advice. I watched him in my mirror, and beads of nervous perspiration blurred his mask of ease. The costumer was pinning ruffles to my unfinished sleeve while asking me if I felt comfortable in shoes two sizes too small. I told him quite honestly that I was a little concerned that my feet had no feeling, but the shoes were fine.

The stage manager gave us our five-minute call in a tone not unlike the summoning of early Christians to the lions. Everyone left hurriedly, except for the talented young actress sharing the table with me. She patted powder onto her makeup, stood, fluffed out her skirt, adjusted her belt, and turned to leave. I still sat staring in the mirror. She put her hand on the back of my chair, leaned forward so I could see her in the mirror, and said, "I admire your guts, lady. That's all it takes to do this."

The show went off well. Strangely enough, during the performance the novice usually comes across better than the regulars because the regulars are so concerned for the newcomer that they lose concentration. Actors secured by many performances will fumble lines, skip speeches, miss exits, and stand awkward and wordless while the underrehearsed substitute steers them gently through a bumbled sequence. The next night, I went back to being the silent understudy and left the regular leading lady to the joy of exercising her "guts."

It isn't easy to perform in public what has been practiced as a standby. For Joshua, that nervousness was magnified by the exalted character of the previous leading man. I think he was scared. God spoke to him in words that comfort all replacements and speak to the deepest needs of any starter under God's assignment. "You may be an extension of Moses, but you are an original Joshua. Your orders are original, your steps are original, your personality is original, and the source of your strength is that which made the originality of Moses valid." Read God's comfort to Joshua. It isn't sugary with sentiment or quivering with doubt. It is certain. "Just as I have been with Moses, I will be with you; I will not fail you or forsake you."³ Great encouragement for Joshua.

Just as God was with Moses, so He was with Joshua . . . and Joshua did well. He led the people into the land prepared for them by the God of Moses and Joshua. And just as God was with Joshua, so He will be with you and me. "I will never leave you or forsake you."⁴

I've been told that in the Greek version of this verse the syntax holds the ultimatum of a triple negative. "I will not, I will not ever, believe Me, I will not relax My grip on you." My security as a believer isn't in the strength of my faith. Nor in the validity of my doctrine. Not even in how many Bible verses I know. All that is wonderful, but my security as a believer rests in His grip on me. *God will not relax His grip!* I've known times when that grip hurt, times when that grip prevented me from running along a self-chosen path, and times when that grip caused me to let go the hold I had on something outside God's will. That grip hasn't always been comfortable, but that grip has been my security.

Travel Tip 4:
You can trust God's plan for your life because He *plants good seed.*

Sometimes I feel I'm missing something, some withheld part that would complete my equipment for living the Christian life. That's when I say, "Lord, if You expect me to do what I sense You directing me to do, You'll have to give me more specialized equipment. That's the problem. Not disobedience but insufficiency!"

How foolish! God never directs us to do what He hasn't already equipped us to do. Everything we are to be is in the seed that God planted at our birth. Usually, we don't recognize the equipment until we step out in obedience, but it's there. The Bible says so.[5]

When I turned my life over to the Lord, I gave Him a list of things I did very well: I had a degree in drama, had a few acting awards to my credit, was considered to be very well-mannered and soft-spoken, and knew which fork to use at a formal dinner. The list included good credit references, books read, and the trait of humility. (I wanted our work together to be productive and made the mistake of thinking that since I knew very little about Him, He knew very little about me.)

I felt sure the traits and track records would let God know how He could best use me. At the same time, I gave Him a short list of things I didn't do well, had no intention of doing and, if asked, would do in such a poor state of fellowship it wouldn't do either one of us any good. To the best of my understanding, He's gotten those lists mixed up!

Most of my Christian life has been spent doing the very things I told Him I wouldn't do. For instance, I told Him I would never give my "testimony" in public. I've always been a very private person and saw no reason to change that pattern. I was willing to accept Jesus in His lordship. I just didn't want others to know it. It seemed to me that if I knew it and God knew it, what business was it to anyone else?

I also told God I wouldn't get mixed up in Bible study. I could tell it was something that might become a habit.

Then, and very carefully, I explained to God that at no time, under any circumstances, would I have anything remotely to do with what was at that time called "religious theater." The groups looked as though they had found an extra striped bathrobe, so they decided to do a play about Joseph. I saw in them no artistry, no disciplined craftsmanship, no ardent professionalism, and certainly no place for me!

Now my life slips easily into categories of activity: I travel and share my testimony, I teach three Bible classes a week, and I'm the full-time director of a Christian theater company. (I've stopped mentioning to God what I won't do, except for a few phrases like, "I will not be a multimillionaire.") Incidentally, the surprise is not that I'm doing what I'm doing, but that I'm enjoying it. God, not I, knew what would give me joy.

There is joy, but often there are times when the task seems to call forth more ability than I have. I expect God to do some strange and foreign thing not in me but to me, some additive of peculiar quality that will enable me to do what has been assigned. How foolish! God plants good seed. The assignment is like an empty flower bed. Don't waste time gazing into *it*. Look at the seed. That little seed is already complete, ready for the process to begin. There is a whole flower in that seed. There is a whole tree in that acorn. God plants good seed and says, "I know the plans I have for you, and they are good." His plans are not diverted by their difficulties; instead, by them, His plans are often defined.

Travel Tip 5:
You can trust God's plan for your life because He *uses broken pieces.*

The goblet in that Steuben glass works ended up in the throwaway bin as broken, discarded fragments. Picture that brown carton of shattered pieces. Does that carton hold any of your dreams, early purposes, highest hopes? Have you felt that God had a plan for you but that you resisted the fire, the design, and His purpose, and there's no place for you but the throwaway bin? I looked in that box of broken glass in the Steuben factory, and I caught a glimpse of me. Me as a runaway. Me refusing the good plan of God. All those baubles and bubbles and blisters of bad glass were me.

"What's good about this news?" I said. "Here I am in God's garbage, the dump box of His creativity."

But wait a minute. The whole story hasn't been told. What happens to that broken glass? It may be that some of it is picked up again in the factory process; I don't know about that. But I do know that something very significant to Christian worship is made from broken glass. Stained-glass windows. The stained-glass window catches the light, and its color deepens with myriad reflections, like a diamond necklace in the moonlight or a fresh dewdrop sparkling in the sun.

God redeems the broken pieces in the throwaway bin, and they become glistening works of art. Even for the brokenhearted there is hope. God can use you. God can use me. There is hope for the broken pieces, and even in hurt, there is the incredible fact of God's hearing our cries of distress.

Travel Tip 6:
You can trust God's plan for your life because *He listens to you.*

It isn't easy getting people's attention these days. One of the most difficult things to teach a young actor is how to maintain active participation in the scene and how to "be there" for the other person as well as speak forth the words of one's own part. Many wives share a common complaint; they married strong, silent types and ended up with men who don't talk. We urge these bashful beloveds to talk primarily to assure us *we* have been heard. The assurance of listening is one of the ways we all fend off the deep fear of isolation.

I fret over the feeling of being passed over. Not heard, not noticed, almost as if I didn't exist. I'll sit in coffee shops waving my empty cup while waitresses pass by me. Clerks in dress shops fall all over themselves greeting someone at the door while I stand planted in the aisle waiting for service. The clerks should notice me. I'm certainly not a mannequin; they don't have them in my size!

One time I went to a beautiful wedding and went down the lengthy receiving line telling each person that the alligators were loose. I politely shook each hand and murmured, "Hello, the alligators are loose."

Nobody said anything. Each of them smiled and handed me to the next person. Finally, one little bridesmaid at the end thanked me and said she had made it herself! Nobody listens.

I played the role of the fortuneteller in Thornton Wilder's magnificent play *The Skin of Our Teeth*. It's a wonderful role full of chanted truths about the dilemma of mankind. At the end of the second act as man climbs into the boat of deliverance from a cataclysmic flood, the fortuneteller stands alone on stage, swagger-hipped, arms akimbo, looking into the audience, and cries, "Nobody listens!"

Does anybody care enough to accept the accountability of hearing? God does! He hears, and He accepts the responsibility for acting on behalf of what He has heard.

If you doubt this, let's look again at Moses' life. He complained to God, "Look at how badly the Hebrew people are being treated—beaten, killed, persecuted. What are You going to do about it?"

God not only answered Moses, He took action. He sent Moses to see Pharaoh, He sent the plagues to convince Pharaoh to change his mind, and He led the people to the Promised Land.

God listens to us today, just as He listened to Moses.

Many years ago, I had a friend in New York who was selected as one of the ten most successful young men in America. A major magazine did a special feature on him, and before the magazine came out, my friend David had lost his job! There was some rearrangement of departmental assignments, and David and his work section were let go.

He was startled but not dismayed, since he had many connections with similar companies and quickly applied for work with them. All of them liked him, respected him, considered him valuable, but none of them had a job for him. For weeks, he followed leads, called company managers, completed interviews. No job available. The casual weeks stretched into months of concern. He regularly collected his unemployment compensation and hoped each week would be the last he would stand in that depressing line.

One day he got to the payment clerk and was handed a slip of paper stamped FUNDS DEPLETED. He walked slowly back to his apartment and thought over the past tedious weeks and months. He was a hard-working young man who had served his company well . . . but was fired. He had been turned down by every firm in his occupation. Some of the rejections had been from friends with tears in their eyes. Now he held a slip of paper saying there were no further funds for his unemployment needs.

As he entered his apartment, David figured how long this last installment of money would last; then he went into his bedroom, knelt by his bed, and cried out to God. David said that in that moment he was enveloped by the joy of a new realization. He, who could not get a job or further compensation, had the incredible experience of being attentively welcomed into the presence of God Himself. He had the ear of almighty God! It was some time before David found suitable work and became reestablished in his profession, but he told me that the victory was in being heard by God when no one else would listen. God not only hears, He takes action on our behalf. In the Bible God says He hears and remembers His covenant. God keeps His word.

Travel Tip 7:
You can trust God's plan for your life because *God keeps His promises.*

God has always done what He said He would do. The first trick that Satan tried was to convince man that God would not do exactly what He said. We've limited Satan's versatility because we're still falling for the same trick. God said, "I remember My covenant, and I will bring you out from under. . . ."[6] And He added, "I will also *redeem* you."[7] The word *redeem* has three major meanings: "to purchase," "to pay for," and "to take off the market." If we are to know the trustworthiness of God, we have to reckon with the whole span of redemption's meaning.

One afternoon I was reading in our living room when I heard a booming burst of sound. I looked out the window expecting to see storm clouds and lightning flashes, but all was calm. I checked in the hall of our apartment to see if any massive change in the building's normal security sent other tenants scurrying to the exits. Nothing—a hall filled with placid emptiness.

I called out to my husband who was spending his Sunday afternoon "fixing things." "What was that?" He always knows what "that" is but isn't always willing to tear himself away from fixing things to give me a full explanation.

"A transformer must have blown," he called out to me from the darkest corner of a closet, contentedly putting a screwdriver and wrench back in their proper places.

The proper spelling of the word *transformer* is all I know about it, so the fact that the transformer had blown didn't give me a detailed reason. Lorraine sensed the gaps in my understanding; he poked his head out from under the heavy, wool-lined overcoat he keeps in his closet, just in case Houston should experience the first blast of our recurring ice age. "You know what a transformer is?"

"Not exactly," I replied.

"Well, all your electrical appliances have to be protected from the full power of the electricity in case there is an overload of voltage." I nodded, my mind already overloaded. Lorraine got to his feet and stood in the closet looking darling with a black coat sleeve dangling over one eye. "This building couldn't handle the full power of all that electricity, so the transformer is there to take that blast of volts." He stepped out of the closet and spread his arms wide. "If the transformer weren't there to take that overload, all your appliances would blow up."

I caught my breath at the picture. A transformer. Arms wide. Taking the full weight of judgment's power so that all of us who are little appliances might be saved. "What happens to the transformer?" I asked.

Lorraine spoke quietly. "It's destroyed by the blast. It has to be taken down." That evening we passed workmen hauling the new transformer into place. High and lifted up!

Jesus Christ died for us. "He was pierced through for our transgressions . . . crushed for our iniquities . . . and by His scourging we are healed"[8] that whosoever (*any* appliance) believes in Him (is under the work of the transformer) will not perish! That's reality! Reality with love. Redemption. Purchased. Paid for. Payment freely given for us.

One year the A.D. Players had a garage sale to raise money. Everybody sold their own things, and they bought everybody else's things. I put my glasses case down, and it sold two times before I could pick it back up! One lady bought a plant and left it on a table while she went to get something else. When she got back, her plant was gone. It had been sold again. She paid for it. She purchased it. But she didn't take it off the market!

If you have believed in Jesus Christ and trusted your life to Him, you have been paid for, purchased, and taken off the market. Never again up for sale. God chooses His words carefully. He has given us the vista of our hope in one encompassing word: *redemption*. We can trust God's plan for us. He packaged it neatly with His infinite knowledge of the past, the present, and the future.

While working on the filming of *Travel Tips From a Reluctant Traveler*, I was, as always, fascinated by the filming process. It's wondrous, and to someone who doesn't understand all its techniques, it's unbelievable. When I could, I walked around the location trying to fathom the matter of each separate work assignment. One day I heard a film director say something that startled me. He was viewing the setup of the next shot as he saw it on a monitoring screen. He saw things he didn't want to appear in the finished scene. He saw things that weren't clear. I looked at the screen and saw blurrings and dots and wobbly lines that weren't true pictures of the scene that was to be filmed.

The director called to his photographer, "Give me confidence. Give me confidence in this shot!" I asked him later to explain what he meant, and he taught me another principle that works in flight.

The director was asking for confidence that the picture he saw was not the picture he would get. "Give me confidence that the reality is not what I see on the screen." That's the picture God's true hope gives us.

I say to God, "God, I'm in flight. I'm out here in the midst of process, and everything doesn't look good to me right now. In fact, a lot of things are wrong with the picture. I want to believe and trust You. Give me confidence in flight that I may trust the celebration."

And God says, "I'll give you a whole book of it. I'll give you the affirmation of My Spirit within you. I'll give you the certainty of the redemption and the power of the person of the Lord Jesus Christ."

Because we know this, we always have hope. We are always ready to celebrate, no matter what the circumstances.

I have a friend whose family grew up in Dallas, Texas, before Dallas was the size it is now. Her grandmother used to wear a full riding attire every time she went to the grocery store. People would laugh at her and tease her. Why did she wear her riding habit to the grocery store? "Because, I love to ride horseback," she answered. "When I go to the grocery store, I always wear my riding outfit just in case somebody will have a horse."

Don't pack up your celebration attire. Don't take off

your party clothes. Have hope. There is going to be a celebration no matter how grim the situation looks right now. In flight, we can be ready to celebrate. Otherwise, when the party comes, we'll be in the wrong clothes. Then we'll have to go all the way back to pick up extra luggage, and we might be too late for the party.

FIVE

Discard Old Luggage Tags

When I first began traveling, I carried far too much luggage, and most of it didn't arrive with me. One friend who was taking me to a plane noticed that little scraps from previous baggage checks were still tied to my suitcase handle. He carefully tore away each remnant of tagging and explained that luggage is sorted by color. A suitcase may get to Memphis by mistake because a scrap of Memphis's destination color is attached to the bag. What a helpful travel tip! I've followed it faithfully ever since.

The same principle affects my journeys in life. Fragments of old destinations can interrupt the progress of my current itinerary, so I need to get rid of those faded fragments—like "If only . . ." and "Why me?" and "They didn't understand"—which will misdirect my luggage and keep me from enjoying the trip. Old luggage tags direct me back to old errors and hurts and embarrassments that don't need a return trip.

Let's look at some of those luggage tags, three common errors that lead us astray: False Expectations, Fantasy Travel, and Foolish Itinerary.

Luggage Tag Remnant 1: False Expectations, a deceptive hint of rosiness that can lead to the blackest despair

---

Many years ago, while living in New York, I heard of the wonderful work being done by a group called Civilian Actress Technicians, theater-trained volunteers who were performing for military outposts throughout the world. A talented roommate of mine had served a year in Tokyo, and through her accounts of that tour of duty, I was attracted by the call of self-sacrificing service. If I remember correctly, I had been out of work for a year, and selling chestnuts in the theater district would have been an appealing job.

Being a Civilian Actress Technician wasn't only a job, it was difficult, faraway, and noble. And it was *theater*. At that time, the greatest need was in Alaska, an area then ungarnished by pipelines or tourists, heaped high with snow, bleakness, and deprivation. I was fascinated. My light case of martyrdom blossomed into full-blown fever. I applied to the Civilian Actress Technicians Service, explaining to my distraught mother and father in Houston that it was a far greater thing that I was doing than I had ever done before.

A few months later, a somewhat inauspicious card announced my acceptance and told me to wait for orders and further information. I prepared as best I could for Alaska. From army surplus stores, I bought a parka, fur-lined boots, and an all-weather coverup that made me look like a militant laundry bag. I went to museums to learn of prehistoric human survival and attended lectures on the Eskimo. I tried to make adjustments to what I thought would be the food of the Klondike. Instead of pastries, I ate snow cones. I weaned myself away from cold drinks by focusing on heavy pottery cups filled with hot chocolate, strong coffee, and chicken broth. (I learned later that there were few chickens in Alaska and that chicken broth there came from the same cylindrical tins as in New York.) The thought of this mighty, frozen, and faraway land frightened me, but I was unswerving in my heroics.

I don't remember where I was when I opened my marching orders, but I know the brown envelope crack-led with official significance. I stood at attention as I pre-pared my eyes, heart, and parka for Alaskan travels. My shoulders were back at an agonizing angle, indicating military readiness. My left arm was swollen from the vari-ous inoculations, and I shivered a bit. It wouldn't be an easy life, but it hadn't been easy for Hannibal or Saint Joan or Admiral Byrd. I unfolded the brown paper, which would announce my arena of service, and read the awe-some words: San Antonio, Texas. San Antonio! Five hours from my Houston home. One of the sunniest, gen-tlest places in the world. What about my parka, mukluks, and dramatic expectations? My military stance dissolved into rag doll shock. I was furious! The letter and my avail-ability crumpled in simultaneous resignation. I quit! The price was too low and therefore beyond my reach. False expectations had violated my nobility. The battle was over before it was joined because the warrior was too weak for a confrontation with obedience.

Expecting Answers According to Your Expectations

The Bible tells a story of a man, Naaman, who was almost betrayed by his false expectations. He was a valiant warrior, a respected leader, and a successful man. Only one thing troubled Naaman's happiness. He was a leper. In the frightening progress of that disease, the respect and success due so valiant a hero would soon crumble into the isolated insignificance of a leper colony.

After one of Israel's frequent wars with Syria, a young Israelite maiden was captured and became a servant to Naaman's wife. She was a wise daughter of Israel who did not let captivity dim her belief in God's power or her compassion for suffering, so she told her mistress of the curative powers of God's prophets back in her homeland.

Naturally, Mrs. Naaman told Mr. Naaman, and he petitioned his boss, the king of Syria, for a curative vacation in Israel's capital, Samaria. The king of Syria knew there were all sorts of cures to be found across the border, so he sent a letter to the king of Israel saying, "Under separate cover, I am sending you Naaman, ten changes of clothing, and $75,000. Please keep the latter two in exchange for curing the former and returning him to me. Sincerely yours, the king of Syria." (The biblical account doesn't give us all these folksy details, but the principle is the same.)[1]

Naaman traveled to see the king of Israel, and the king of Israel went to pieces. (He went through the ten changes of clothing like three housewives at a garage sale.)

"I can't cure this leper," he wept, palming the $75,000 as he blotted his tears with the Syrian king's letter. "This is all a trick so Syria can start another war."

In the midst of his histrionics, we note that anytime the right message is given to the wrong man, the recipient is likely to go to pieces. A king may be a good king, an accountant may be a good accountant, a mother may be a good mother, and a husband may be a good husband, but if you ask of them more than they've been given, they'll fall like a headless coat hanger under the weight of your dependence. God never asks the baker to mend His shoes or the cobbler to bake His bread, but we often dump the right message on the wrong desk and are bewildered by the consequences.

Such tragedies thread through our society offering glaring pictures of human ruin: children crippled for life because they were overloaded with the responsibility of keeping their parents' marriage together, pastors defecting valid ministries because their churches ask them to be all things to so many people that they become nothing to anyone, teachers drained and unproductive because their students' parents demand that the classroom do the work only a family at home can do. Are apple trees uprooted because they produced no pecans? No! The king of Israel wasn't a prophet of God, and the message for the prophet sent him into shock.

The news of the king's distress reached the ears of Israel's true prophet, Elisha, who sent a message to the robe-rending ruler. "Don't tear up those clothes. We can use them in the thrift shop! Send Naaman to me. God will show His hand through His appointed prophet."

The king of Israel was delighted to get Naaman off his agenda, and Naaman was delighted to get off the king's doorstep. He didn't really care who cured his leprosy. He just wanted to go back home in good, healthy condition, so he hightailed it to Elisha's house. It wasn't easy turning that caravan around, something like backing an eighteen-wheeler into a curved driveway. You see, Naaman traveled in style. He was a prominent Syrian under the king's special attention and was accompanied by a liveried entourage much like the first two blocks of a Macy's parade. I can imagine attendants preceding, walking beside, and following Naaman.

The first group announced to passers-by, "Naaman is coming. Naaman is coming."

The second group sang little ditties proclaiming, "Naaman is here! Here is Naaman!"

The third group trotted in his wake saying, "You just missed Naaman."

He rode in a black sling-back carriage that slid through the winding streets of Samaria like an ebony slipper on freshly waxed floors. The only thing more flamboyant than Naaman's accouterments is my imagination in describing them. Naaman, the patient, approached the gate of Elisha, the doctor-prophet. Naaman, announced, heralded, and double-parked. Naaman, pompous, assured, and desperately sick.

Did Elisha rush to welcome Naaman into his office? Did Naaman get double-promoted past all the others in the waiting room? Did Elisha contact the morning show, news at noon, and the *Samaria Sentinel* so the world would know a wonderful healing was to be done? No.

A messenger, not even the prophet himself, came to the gate, cracked it open a few inches, stared at the waiting assembly, and muttered, "Go and wash in the Jordan seven times, and your flesh will be restored to you, and you shall be clean."

Wash in the Jordan seven times? That's like a neurosurgeon leaving a message on his answering service, "Take two aspirin and call me in the morning."

Naaman was furious! Angry, humiliated, proud, and unhealed, he left muttering to himself, "This country bumpkin doesn't seem to know who I am! And I expected a great show of healing, waving his hands, calling on the name of his Lord, and a little soul-stirring music! What a waste this trip has been!"

Why did Naaman leave without the healing? Because his luggage was tagged with false expectations. He wanted to be healed, but he wanted to be healed in the way he expected to be healed. He expected the panacea of pandemonium, not a prosaic prescription. His eyes and heart were tuned for religious fervor and spectacle, not the pale absurdity of simple obedience. False expectations can invalidate any trip.

Mr. Naaman had a good servant who ran to him and said, "Sir, if the prophet had told you to do some great thing, you would have done it. All he says is to wash and be clean. Try it. You might like it."

Naaman did, and guess what happened? He was cured. He was clean! But he almost missed it through false expectations.

Don't risk detours because false expectations still cling to your luggage. The Christian journey can be valid with inauspicious beginnings. Often the hardest thing is that first small step of basic obedience. I've seen gallant Christians falter because they refused to join a church. I've seen ministries crumble because it was easier to dress up for the parade than to dress down to clean the bathrooms. I've seen commitment lose its voice when the first word was *obedience*. And I've also been troubled by Naaman's first error in what he expected. He expected the king to serve as prophet. I, too, know the error of holding the wrong people accountable for my answers. Let me give you an illustration in case you might have some old tags like it.

Holding People Accountable
for Your Answers

I was given a wonderful opportunity to spend a little time with a prominent Christian philosopher, a wise and gifted writer whose words had been the first to jab through the maze of questions and hostilities in my unbelief. Now I would meet with him, talk with him, ask him the questions that tumbled under the peaceful bedspread of my contrived contentment. Now I could recite the catechism of my perplexity and receive the clarification of his certainty.

I didn't want to waste one second of the opportunity. I rejected my peripheral questions. This wasn't the time for idle chatter. I trimmed away the echoes of other people's queries; they would have to wait for their own day in his presence. I focused on a major conundrum.

For months one question had been uppermost in my mind: What really matters in life? If Christ was uniquely sovereign, all the disciplinary choices I had to make each day because He was Lord of my life were valid. If not, these choices were foolish at best because they required so much of me.

We met! The great man and our party for a quiet dinner together. I loved him. His eyes glowed with each intake of breath. When he spoke to one of us, he tilted his head as a halo-haired owl, focused in concerned attention. Each of us caught the glow of wisdom and became apprentice sages, sitting comfortably at his feet.

Later we gathered for dialogue. He lavished attention on each question, smiling at the questioner as though together they were tasting a new caviar and found it wonderful. I waited my turn. I didn't want my question to piggyback. I wanted it to share its serving of wisdom with none other.

89

When I finally spoke, I was very clear. First, I thanked him for what his writing had done for me. It felt good to express my gratitude, a kind of easing release. Then, almost tasting the moment, I asked my question. "What to you is unique about Christ?"

He didn't understand.

I clarified.

He didn't understand.

Others clarified. They understood, but he didn't.

Then, slipping into the library of his wisdom, he thought a moment in silence.

I waited, honored by his thoughtfulness.

He shrugged. "It doesn't matter," he said and went on to the next question!

I couldn't believe it. The light at the end of the tunnel went out! This gentle giant of Christian counsel had no answer for me!

Afterward, I realized that he had an answer. The answer I needed. I was holding his wisdom accountable for my answer, and in his dismissal, he answered me. Mine hadn't been an honest, open question. It was a manipulated query, seeking to confirm what I didn't have enough faith to believe. Like Elijah, I listened through the wind and earthquake and fire only to hear God in the articulate silence. Faith is evidence that dwells comfortably where the answers are mute.

God doesn't take away the miracle of our thinking process. He weans us away from the certainty of wise men so we might stretch our own understanding and stand on tiptoe to touch the lower stars of personal discovery. There is wisdom to be found in, "And what do *you* think?" That is an answer. God would have us know the process of personal discernment. Rembrandt once told a demanding student, "First put well into practice what you already know. In time, you will learn those hidden things about which you now inquire."

Unfortunately, most of us want answers given quickly, in neat, claimable packages. We are hungry only for fast-food wisdom. We want our pulpits to serve Jack-in-the-box theology and deliver instant understanding so that our faith may claim immediate ease. God, on the contrary, teaches that there is no fast route to discernment. We must walk, step by step, the pilgrimage of study, practice, and time.

Seek Wisdom in Study. I don't find Bible study easy. I know many people who do, and I rejoice with them in their lighthearted assimilation of God's Word. There are times when I'm preparing for my 8:00 P.M. Bible class, and at 7:00, I'm bewildered, even though I'm surrounded by notebooks, commentaries, and dictionaries. Instead of getting my notes together, I'm trying to think of a logical reason to cancel. I must look foolish to God when I'm faithlessly fuming and fretting over a lesson on faith.

Studying the Bible is a lot like eating pecans, those giant paper shell prides of Texas. You can crack them in your hand and eat the fat, sweet meat that falls easily from the shell. Often that is how I feast on God's Word, with the accessible truths smiling up at me from the printed page. Other times, Bible study isn't so simple.

Just like eating a pecan. One half slides easily from the shell. The other half crumbles, and little pieces hide in the fragile chambers of the shell. You scrape at it with your fingernail, pound it against the heel of your hand trying to shake it free. It takes a little work, maybe even the probing of a silver nutmeat picker, but that morsel of nutmeat is worth the extra effort. It might be even sweeter than the half that fell out so easily.

There are many methods available to us for Bible study: church study groups, taped lectures, informal classes in homes, the recent availability of Bible study programs on film, such as the series on which this book is based (the four-part film series "Travel Tips from a Reluctant Traveler," produced by White Lion Pictograph, San Antonio, Tex.). The simplest way to learn is in a class under a strong teacher, but there can be no learning without energetic activity on the part of the learner.

Scripture provides a working recipe for learning: "Make your ear attentive to wisdom, incline your heart to understanding. For if you cry for discernment and lift your voice for understanding; *if you seek her as silver, and search for her as for hidden treasures; then you will discern the fear of the* LORD, *and discover the knowledge of God."*[2] God gives wisdom, but we must seek it as actively as we look for hidden treasure. We will never be wise if we know only the reflection of other people's wisdom.

Has your trip been detoured by false expectations? Did you expect the right answer from the wrong person or deny a godly opportunity because it wasn't packaged as you designed? Don't be threatened by wayward luggage venturing toward old errors.

Travel Tip:
Throw away the old luggage tags of false expectations.

Luggage Tag Remnant 2: Fantasy Travel, a lackluster shade of fading green, which leads us away from the vibrant hue of reality

One of my favorite parables is the story of the wheat and tares.[3] Jesus tells of a farmer who faithfully planted good wheat in his field. He did his job well, but while he slept, the enemy planted tares, unwanted grass resembling wheat but not of its value. A mighty principle is given as in the similarity between the worthy and the unworthy. Only as the wheat grew were the tares evident; then the farmer saw the tares usurping the ground, food, and growing rights of the good wheat.

When we find similar circumstances in our lives, we blunder into a foolish indictment of the whole field. We cry out, "The field is worthless!" and settle down into despair. Our fantasy travel leads us away from options for produce. Confrontation with growing tares is a cue not for defeat but for endurance in hope.

Let me give you an illustration from a theater discipline: the art of pantomime. The great mimes cause empty space to become what they would have us see. A gesture in space becomes a pole. A flick of the fingers becomes an umbrella. An eyebrow raised gives us two people in dialogue on a crowded, rain-drenched street, where in reality there is only one small figure on an empty stage. Such is the dynamic of pantomime.

Working with this medium, I've learned what can be done and also what cannot be done, at least what cannot be done by lesser skills than those of the expert. Picture a mime eating an ice-cream cone. See his tongue lick around the oozing circle of the frozen cream. As you watch and taste, you think, *Surely, it's butter pecan. In fact, Blue Bell's butter pecan.*

As you watch the mime, you see the cone, feel it in your hand, and taste the ice cream. You see the cone softening at the top as the rich delicacy spills over your fingers wound around its stem. You feel the moist sweetness clinging to your lips. So you press your lips together to draw in the taste, and one small dollop of pecan clings to the corner of your mouth. You don't waste it! Quickly, your tongue delivers it to your mouth.

The magic of belief encircles the mime. The ice-cream treat is real.

Until someone enters with an ice-cream cone in *fact*, not in fantasy. This ice-cream cone is different. It is larger in real life. The ice cream clings to the cone, almost an expression of resistance to the lazy licking of the eater. Spilling is not so delicate on the fingers; the fingers don't accept the stickiness so readily. The cone, as it crumbles, requires a shifting of the hand, which the fantasy treat did not effect. The reality has revealed the inadequacy of the fantasy. *The good wheat reveals the tares!*

You may have reckoned with the tares in your life and deemed the whole field worthless. You may have risked one quick realistic appraisal of the world you loved and trusted and, in that appraisal, have been forced to admit there is something definitely rotten in your Denmark. You may have even had to deal with the fact that not all Christians are perfect, as you expected them to be.

Let me give you some good news. God knows more about the tares than you do, and He still loves the field! Judgment is not your responsibility. It is uniquely God's. If there are tares growing in your garden, you may have the opportunity to weed them out. Withdrawal is not the answer. Let me tell you how I dealt with the tares of fantasy travel during a retreat I attended in California.

Weeding Out the Fantasy

I thought I came to the meeting with a holy attitude of righteous and efficient service. I was to be the speaker for a large conference of women in an indescribably beautiful retreat center. Everything about the planning and planting looked good to me and for me. However, I soon learned otherwise.

I spoke the first of three scheduled times but didn't speak well. My notes, which had been wonderfully appropriate in my study at home, were no more relevant to the conference's theme than my tailored suit, evening dress, and high-heeled shoes were to the casual dress of the conferees. Three people had greeted me with the loud love of bosom buddies, and I couldn't recall or recognize any one of them. The miniworkshop for which I had prepared a careful consideration of how to develop a drama ministry in the church was announced as "How to Exercise One's Gift of Hospitality." (I don't understand the term *miniworkshop*. Every conference has them. They require major preparation, take up the entire afternoon, and are compared with no other workshop of varying size but are always called "mini.")

The attractive young woman in charge of transportation informed me that the closing meeting had been changed to a later time. Since I couldn't meet my scheduled departure, I would be taken to a shuttle flight early the next morning, contradicting my original itinerary. "It's all a part of God's good plan," she said cheerfully, "so, of course, you don't mind."

I minded! I also doubted it was part of God's good plan. If it was, I wasn't.

Weakened by the effort of smiling when there was no trace of joy in my heart, I flopped down on the bed in my room and was engulfed by dust from the faded bedspread. I cried! Yes, I, noble saint of the speakers' bureau, wept. I was angry with the circumstances, disappointed with myself, and uneasy in my relationship with God.

My second speech was to be, believe it or not, "Joy Under Pressure." Don't tell me God doesn't have a sense of humor! There was no way I could handle that topic. I was too sanctimonious to admit to pressure and too miserable to remember joy. All I knew was that somehow I had once again failed to be the person I should have been. That was the moment when the "event" came into being. I had to deal with the tares in my life. I had to cancel my ticket for fantasy travel. It was necessary for my personal survival.

I conducted, there in my room, a funeral service. Yes, a funeral service. I placed the room's one chair so that I might sit and grieve over the pretended coffin of the beloved departed. In silence, I remembered all that I had loved about her. Then I stood and, with bowed head and many tears, spoke a few words of appropriate eulogy.

She, the deceased, was a wonderful person, perfect in every way. She was exactly what the conference had wanted. She never spoke without spectacular effectiveness. No one moved during her illustrative anecdotes, except to regain their attentiveness after the laughter that followed all her jokes. The conference leaders gazed upon her wide-eyed. Everything she said was clinically relevant. Everyone took notes, even the groundskeeper who listened from outside the window. As she concluded, there was a clatter of pencils dropped as all in attendance jumped to their feet with tumultuous applause and appropriate praises to God. Half the group made conversion decisions, including the groundskeeper who resolved to go back to the wife and four children he had abandoned to run off with a blonde barmaid (who would also ultimately convert after listening to the tapes of the one so properly eulogized).

This noble one, so abruptly deceased, always wore exactly the right clothes and never brought more luggage than was absolutely necessary. She remembered everybody's name and instinctively knew what personal dilemmas needed healing words from her lips. She cared not a slivered whit if her travel plans were changed because she never doubted God's hand, and besides that, she was an expert pilot with an uncanny access to a Lear jet, regardless of how remote the location might be. She never grumbled. She never wept, except for others. She was never angry, and she traveled with a small collapsible broom and wet mop so she might tidy up and make beautiful any place she stayed.

As I eulogized, I realized how devotedly I admired this lady. Her name, of course, was Jeannette (never misspelled, incidentally). She was in critical need of burial. She didn't exist. She was a fantasy. A creation of the tare of pride. I wept over her. I grieved for her. And in the presence of God who had created me, I buried her. Then I washed my face and removed the streak marks of tears well spent. I took off my suit jacket and put on a sweater, which had nothing remotely in common with the skirt, slipped into tennis shoes, and walked down the hill to the next meeting. The rest of the conference wasn't perfect, but it was wonderful—filled with the wonder of reality accepted.

Unfortunately, that fabulous fantasy of Jeannette has a strong spirit. She frequently resurfaces, clawing her way out of her grave with perfectly manicured nails to challenge my right to exist. Her funerals are frequent and costly. But they are always necessary. Poor dear, she just had another. When that ghost reappears, I remember that the God of Abraham, Isaac, and Jacob is indeed the God of reality. The right to celebrate in flight requires a recognition of reality.

I've made mistakes. I must confront them and, where I can, correct them. I can even lean on them to help me understand my fellow travelers in flight, but they have no authority over me. The Lord of the wheat field knows the way of the tares. He also knows He has planted good seed . . . and its time, too, has come.

Travel Tip:

Recognize the tares, but celebrate the wheat. Remember, what might have been *never was!*

Luggage Tag Remnant 3: Foolish Itinerary

Have you ever traveled with someone who never saw a new place and was never satisfied with the itinerary? This person always finds some fault in the sights. The Atlantic misses the accessibility of his backyard swimming pool. The Mississippi doesn't flow quickly like the Guadalupe. The Alps aren't red like the mountains in Colorado. The Louvre is less focused than the art class textbook. The world in all its wonders is dimmed by such unfair comparisons. No itinerary satisfies.

However, great beauty is seen with the heart as well as the eyes. My friends Hazel and Howard Goddard love their home in Colorado, so when they see the Alps, the Alps will have a little of Colorado in it. I love the Texas hill country, so when I stand awed by the grandeur of Mount Hood, my heart sees a little of the gentle hills around Kerrville, Texas. That is not denying the experience; it is identifying it by one's experience.

Instead, the insatiable itinerary demands that the Alps be something they are not! It demands that Borger, Texas, produce edelweiss. It is living one's life saying satisfaction can be realized only by the ultimately impossible. It is demanding the said to become unsaid, the done to become never done, and the hurt—not healed—but never to have happened!

My mother was asked what she wanted to do on her ninetieth birthday. She thought a moment and then, with one finger punctuating the air, said, "Live and let live—and take a good nap." Amen and amen! Wise southern lady, she knew that an insatiable itinerary can ruin the trip, and it can interfere with your right to celebrate. You and I can't change people and most places. Allow the Alps to be the Alps; Roach, Missouri, to be Roach, Missouri; and Leakey, Texas, to be Leakey, Texas. Allow the itinerary its integrity. Your heart might have two places to love instead of one.

Desiring What You Cannot Have

The book of Proverbs addresses the dilemma of foolish itineraries. A greedy man had two daughters, "Gimme" and "Gimmee." Greediness isn't always taught by greedy parents, but it's no surprise to see children learning from what they see their parents do rather than what their parents tell them to do. I can imagine that these daughters saw their father grasping for what wasn't his, begging for what he hadn't earned, and wanting what he didn't need. He probably berated heaven for giving him demanding daughters, "What did I do that I might have children who drain me of everything I've got?" What did he do? He trained them. I can imagine that they saw him never satisfied and became what they saw.

The story ends with the words, "There are three things that will not be satisfied, four that will not say, 'Enough.' "[4] These things have focused their demands on what cannot be, and thus, all that *can* be is dissatisfaction. The three things are Sheol, which never closes its gates, earth, which never quenches its thirst, and fire, which never has enough fuel.

The other listing focuses on a womb that is barren. This barren womb craves the children it cannot have. You say this doesn't speak to you because you don't yearn for the patter of little feet. You're quite content honoring God without the joy of 3:00 A.M. feedings, frantic calls through the list of baby sitters, the all-night parental watch for teenage dates, the high cost of college tuition, and the trauma of wedding bills. Think again. Have you defined your happiness as getting some treasure you don't have? Have you said you will never be happy until you are married or divorced or the head of the company or vacationing in Bermuda?

I tried to comfort a young woman whose fiancé had broken their engagement the afternoon of what was supposed to be their wedding day. I wept with her, heard her pain, assured her that her anger was reasonable, and listened in silence as she went over and over the shocking details of her broken heart. The break in their relationship hadn't been recent. The incident, in fact, had happened over two years before our talking of it. I marveled that she was still so paralyzed with grief until I heard her say, "I don't want God's best for my life. I want Ray to come back."

I sat at the bedside of a lovely Christian lady who was suffering physically from a deep emotional hurt. Her husband had thoughtlessly worded his will in such a way that her right to their home was in question. At her husband's death, she had been well provided for; every financial need was met. She was loved, cared for, and attended by her many friends and large family, but none of that mattered. She had literally made herself ill by demanding one thing only of God: that her husband's will be changed. A foolish itinerary to chart: demanding that the said become unsaid and the done become undone.

I talked to a young man whose life was rich with opportunity. He was healthy and mentally capable of splendid work in his chosen field, but his future was squandered on a deeply rooted bitterness toward his father. He craved only one thing: to hear his father confess the deeds of bad parenting.

A stated dependence on reactions over which we have no authority dooms us to an appetite that knows no satisfaction. The parent who demands that a child's career choice meet the parent's unrealized dreams, the sister who thinks of nothing other than her bitterness toward an unloving sister—all are pursuing foolish itineraries. Have you held someone else accountable for your happiness? Have you kept hurts from healing so the one responsible must pay for your suffering?

I've learned we frequently relinquish misery only when we feel it has served its purpose, and I grieve that we often deal with misery indefinitely because we demand the impossible for its surcease. The barren womb dependent upon the children it cannot produce. The itinerary blocked by its insatiable appetite.

Travel Tip:
Tear up that foolish itinerary and chart a realistic course.

Do I still have to deal with lost luggage? Yes, occasionally. Even the best airlines send an overnight case to distant lands that humans can't find overnight. But I figure I'm not going to help them lose it.

Check your luggage tags. The proper tag will take you to a new world of great, joyous difference.

SIX

Learn How to Get
Back on Track

I was speaking at a women's conference several years ago, and the lady who introduced me was lovely, energetic, and at ease. I couldn't even match her two out of three. I was travel worn, tired, and uncomfortable. She said, "Isn't it wonderful that Christians don't have problems?"

I thought, *Well, you do now, because I'm your speaker . . . and I have problems.*

Somewhere in our energetic denial of problems, we Christians have given the impression that dilemmas deny our relationship with God.

Often we walk around oblivious to our problems as I did one day, not very long ago, in Boca Raton, Florida. It was a lovely event. I tried to look my best for the speaking engagement by wearing a black knit suit with a little pearl pin. My talk that morning went well. Afterward, some sponsors of the event took me around to see Boca

Raton. As we moved from shop to shop, I noticed out of the corner of my eye that one lady would come toward our group and then turn around and leave.

We'd go to another area, and she'd come to the group and then slip away. I'm very shy and, therefore, sensitive to people who are shy, so I tried to smile her into the group. *God might have spoken to that lady while I was talking*, I thought. *Maybe I'll have a chance to continue that special conversation*. But my smile didn't seem to encourage her to join us.

The next time we turned a corner and the lingering lady approached us, I left the group and went around behind her.

"Hi!" I said.

"Oh, uh, could I talk to you for just a minute?" she asked.

"Certainly."

We went over to an area in a little bookstall, which was very private, and I said to her, "What was it you wanted to say?"

"I uh, I uh, I wanted . . ." She stopped, eyes downcast, the middle fingers of her right hand pressed to her lips.

I had seen that pose so many times. Hurting, bewildered people trying to check the pain, which will finally burst out in words long withheld. I thought, *Bless her heart*, and put my arm around her. "Honey, tell me. It can't be this bad. Tell me."

"Well, I just wanted to tell you . . . that your skirt is on inside out."

The dilemma was no longer hers. It was mine! I had been walking around Boca Raton, Florida, with a little tag on my right hip telling everyone how to wash me! I thought I had my act together, but my best was inside out. This kind lady was right to help me see that I had the problem, not her.

I've found that trials and tribulations often define my relationship with God because we know the certainty of Christ's faithfulness as He carries us through our problems.

BE PREPARED FOR DILEMMAS

The Christian life is joyous. However, it isn't always easy. The route of the sanctified life hasn't necessarily been set apart from trials and tribulations. Or, at least, it hasn't been for me.

One morning I was on my way to work after a previous day that had been very difficult. Months earlier, I had taken an executive training seminar. The consultants had advised, "In times of stress, remove everything that is not urgent from your desk." I had, but it hadn't made any difference.

I'd decided to leave home an hour early that morning so I could get started on the remnants of yesterday's work, but that seemed a hopeless cause. Traffic was bad. The car in front of me was driving too close to me. I cried out, *Oh, Lord! Slow everything down*.

I realized God would say to me, *Jeannette, don't ask Me to slow down the rapids. The nature of the rapids is that they are rapid*. God's action toward us isn't always to change the nature of our dilemma. Instead, He gives us principles that work within the dilemma, principles to keep us afloat in the rapids. Again we will call them "travel tips."

Before we talk about those principles, however, let's look at some of the dilemmas we encounter.

As a Bible teacher, I've looked vainly for Hebrews in the Old Testament. In front of my class! As a platform speaker, I've spoken in error—and on tape, too. As a wife, I've stormed at my husband for not mailing the invitations I forgot to give him. Minor errors. I've also committed major errors, inadmissible even in this telling, errors compounded by my avoiding their responsibility. It seems that the older we get, the harder it is to say, "I was wrong. I made a mistake."

Dilemmas Caused by Our Error

It isn't easy to confront and confess our personal accountability in dilemmas that hurt us and others. I've awakened at two in the morning, praying that I didn't say the words I remember myself saying so clearly. My blunders are seldom mumbled. Instead, they are said distinctly with all in attendance listening! Voice projection is such a problem when I'm saying my words correctly, but not when, in one performance, I said, "The Romans *is* coming!" Apparently, everyone in the world heard that.

The people who smile and say, "We all make mistakes," usually mean "*you* all" and not "*me* all."

I've sat with unhappy couples and marveled at how articulate each one is in pronouncing the other's errors, yet neither one can manage the simple phonetics of "I was wrong." At other times, I realize that the one who slips most easily into the *mea culpa* of full responsibility is silently convinced of his innocence.

Dilemmas Beyond Ourselves

We are also affected by dilemmas not composed of our mistakes but made up of circumstances and crises over which we have little or no control: sudden economic reversal not attributable to our manner of addressing job assignments, illnesses and accidents that have no evidence of personal irresponsibility, major decisions added to our agenda already overloaded with stress. The choices we make in such chaos reflect how well we have made Christian principles a part of our automatic reflexes. In each, there is opportunity, but in each, there may also be the pain of helpless feelings. I'm convinced that nothing gets to the believer that doesn't have to get past God first. I know that, and I claim that stabilizing fact.

Dealing with Dilemmas

We make strange choices in dealing with dilemmas. Often those choices are out of character. For instance, me. I try to avoid dilemmas. I ignore them. I run from them. Yet, sometimes there are benefits in dilemmas, bonus principles I learn as I struggle through an ordeal. If I could only realize dilemmas as benefits, I wouldn't miss a one.

After all, I usually hate to miss out on any benefits. I never check out from a hotel without taking the complimentary shower cap and unused soap. (In fact, I often choose hotels because of the niceties of the extras.) The tiny packages of sewing essentials go into my purse before I unpack my makeup kit. (By the way, those sewing kits have recently included two small Band-Aids, which precisely cover the pricks in my thumb regularly caused by my essential sewing. Thank you, Mr. and Mrs. Taiwan.) I've been known to keep a Holiday Inn bellman waiting for my check-out while I crawled under the bed to retrieve my favorite Sheraton Grand ballpoint pen. The two plastic vials of shampoo and conditioner are added to the shelves in my bathroom, already filled with the bounty from previous trips. Despite diets and abundant banquets, my attitude toward the good-night chocolate left on my pillow is similar to that of the mountain climber who climbs a new mountain. I eat it "because it's there." I hate to miss any benefits.

Why would I overlook the benefits that can come from going through—not running away from—dilemmas? Once I finally asked myself this question, I learned to deal with dilemmas of all sizes in fellowship with God who is all abundance. I don't want to miss any divine benefits!

The Israelites' Dilemma

I often turn to two passages in the Bible that illustrate our choices in dilemmas. One tells the incredible story of Israel at the border of the Promised Land.[1] God had specified this land's boundaries to Abraham, had called, trained, and cued Moses to lead the way out of Egypt, and had poured miracles upon those wayfarers—the opening of the Red Sea, the pillar of cloud by day and of fire by night, the marvel of manna, and the water flowing from the riven rock. God's people stood at the border of the Holy Land. It was there and in sight! A land flowing with milk and honey to be claimed by an obedient people.

God directed that spies be sent into Canaan so the people might taste and see God's goodness and fully understand His work. God had even given a clear account of how the land would be occupied in spite of those Hivites, Canaanites, and Hittites who had settled as usurpers in Israel's God-given territory. He said, "I will drive them out before you *little by little*, until you become fruitful and take possession of the land."[2]

That "little by little" is hard for us to hear. We want it done in a hurry. Whether it be territory in land or territory in our personal lives, we want it cleared out and ready in an instant. But process is God's honorable laboratory.

Israel's spies found the land richer than they had dreamed it would be. When they got to the valley of

Eshcol, they chopped down a branch with a single cluster of grapes, which was so large it took two men to carry it on a pole between them. (If you visit Israel today, you will see the insignia of grapes carried by two men, denoting the abundance of provision in this wonderful land.)

When the spies returned to Moses and the congregation of Israel, they announced, "The land certainly does flow with milk and honey, and this is its fruit." God's promise validated by evidence you could see, touch, smell, and taste. All was as God had said it would be.

Nevertheless, there is always a human "nevertheless." How often we refute God's benevolence with our interpolated "nevertheless"! The spies gave out a bad report because they saw strong people in the land (just as God had said) with fortified cities (just as God had said) and the descendants of Anak (just as God had said). Interesting, when they abandoned the details of God's overview, they abandoned the view of overcoming!

Caleb and Joshua urged the people to move as God had commanded, but the bad report from the other spies was too much for Israel's stomach. They formed a committee to quit. And God said He would let the quitters quit! He abandoned Israel to wander aimlessly in the desert until that unbelieving generation died off. Only Caleb and Joshua would live to lead the new generation into the land that had been ready ever since the Exodus from Egypt.

Harsh ending to a gallant parade? Not really. Instead, an awesome example of the patience of God. The people had practiced quitting from the Red Sea's borders. They continually muttered, "You have brought us out into this wilderness to kill this whole assembly with hunger"[3] or thirst or weariness. Over and over again, they cried, "We will quit and go back to Egypt."

What was the terror in the spies' report that led the

people to quit and finally back down from claiming the ready promise of God? Ten of the spies cried out, "We saw the inhabitants of the land as giants and saw ourselves as grasshoppers."[4] Let me assure you, when we consider the enemy a giant and ourselves as grasshoppers, the enemy always agrees. If you see your dilemma as beyond the hand of God, the dilemma is delighted. The enemy will never correct your error. Why should he? His strength is in the error of fear's viewpoint. His weakness is in the fact of God. Results of that battle at the border of Canaan: Giants 40, Grasshoppers 0.

Travel Tip:
Align your assessment with God's, and His grasshoppers will be stronger than the enemy's giants.

The Bible is not a story of people who lacked dilemmas, as some Christians like to think. Instead, it is a history of people who dealt with their problems in God's power. Look at an example in the lives of Jesus' disciples.

The Disciples' Dilemma

After the feeding of the five thousand, the disciples got into a small boat and started to row across the Sea of Galilee. The weather was calm when they started out, but a sudden storm swept that small body of water, and the winds and waves slapped against that boat. It was dark. It was stormy. The men were terrified.

In my dilemmas, I identify with the men in the boat. It doesn't take much darkness and storm and angry winds to terrify me. I'm probably the only Houstonian for whom a hurricane alert is a wasted announcement. I'm always on hurricane alert! I've been living in a state of alert ever since I experienced my first hurricane. I see myself in the terror of those fishermen. They tried their best to handle the situation, but they weren't getting anywhere. In my mind, their oars weren't even touching the water. Have you ever done your best, without getting *any*where?

Soon after I turned my life over to the Lord, I expected such wonderful things to happen. I expected smooth sailing.

And things got turbulent. I said, "Lord, I'm doing my best. I'm working as hard as I can, but things are getting bad, and I might get discouraged. God, I don't want to disturb You. But if I get real discouraged, I might quit."

Have you ever threatened God with your weakness? I said, "Lord, if it doesn't get better, I'll really quit."

And things got worse. I worked harder. I said, "Lord, I know to what lengths You went to get me into the fellowship. And I know You're depending on me. So don't put too much stress on me. I might give up."

Still things got worse.

One morning I really couldn't deal with it. I said, "God, I want to be honest with You. I've done the best I can. But I haven't had any encouragement. I'm really despairing. I've warned You. God, I quit!"

And there was this tremendous sigh of relief from heaven! Finally, God had Jeannette where He could do through her what she was trying to do for Him all by herself. Maybe those fishermen were ready for the same lesson.

It's interesting that the most public display of Christ's power immediately preceded the disciples' dilemma. Do you remember the story? Christ was teaching them. And there was a great crowd gathered. He realized they were hungry. He turned to Philip who lived in that area and said, "Is there any place around here where these people can be fed?"

"There's no place here that could feed this many people," Philip answered.

Jesus asked the other disciples, "What do you have?"

Like us, they kept telling Him what they didn't have. "Well, we don't have a place large enough to feed all these people. Even if we had a place large enough to feed all these people, it'd be closed because this is a holy day. Even if there were a place large enough to feed all these people, and it were open, we don't have enough money. We only have a handful of pennies." A handful of pennies!

Oh, every time I think of that I'm reminded of myself. You know, if you've got a lot of extra prayer time, it's quite all right to tell Him what you can't do. It gives you a good feeling of dialogue. But if you have to be economical about your prayer time, don't waste it by telling God what you can't do. He's really not interested. He's only interested in what you're willing to let Him do through you.

So Jesus looked at them, and He made what I think is one of His most significant remarks. He said to them, "Don't send these people away hungry. You feed them. *You* feed them."

I hear that in my stomach where fear is knotted. I know my limited capacity, yet I hear His limitless assignment. "You with your doubts and your list of inadequacies. You with that pitiful clutch of pennies. *You* feed the multitude!"

I can imagine that the disciples all got together. (We often cluster in bewilderment at God's assignment.) Peter said, "What do you suppose He's trying to do?"

Andrew said, "I don't know, maybe it's an object lesson. But I can't even think about it because this little kid keeps pulling on me, trying to give me his lunch."

Matthew, the accountant, was counting the people, "Ten, twenty, thirty, forty."

Thomas said, "Some good may come out of this, but I doubt it."

Finally, Jesus said, "What do you have?"

And they said, "We don't have anything. We've got this little kid who's trying to give us his lunch. But what good would that do?"

"Well, bring that to Me." So they brought the little boy's lunch to Jesus. And He thanked God for it.

Incidentally, have you ever thought the little boy's mother was probably in that group out there? Can you imagine? She had packed that lunch. She knew what was in there, and she also knew what was not there. Can't you imagine her eyes riveted to the little supply of food? Left-over food, at that.

Then Jesus called the disciples to Him, and He told them to tell everybody to sit down in an orderly way. He gave each disciple a little handful of crumbs and fish and said, "Take this to the people."

"You obey Me," Jesus said. Sometimes I answer, "Lord, I would obey You, and I would do what You tell me to do. But I'm not going to be able to pull it off, and both of us will look bad." Have you ever tried to protect almighty God so that He won't get a bad mark for your inadequacies?

I identify with the disciples. Can you imagine Peter? He had all those rows he was going to feed, and there was a row waiting for him to begin. He looked down in his hands. He had maybe the tail end of a little dried fish and two little crumbs. And he looked at a man, and he said, "When I give you this, look fed."

Andrew, over on his side of the crowd, said, "When I serve this, chew slowly."

Matthew was counting the fragments, "One, two, three."

Thomas was saying, "This may work out, but I doubt it."

Finally, Peter did the most marvelous thing. He did what Jesus said! He began to feed the people. And as the disciples handed out the food, it multiplied in their hands. Peter handed out a little crumb, and he had more than he had when he started. He handed that out, and he had still more. He handed that out, and he had more than he could hold. He yelled, "Hey, Andy! Come over here!"

Andrew said, "I don't have time. You won't believe what's happening over here!"

Matthew was counting, "One, two, three."

Thomas said, "It may be food, but I doubt it."

Incredible! They saw Him feed the multitude. And the next time we hear of them, the disciples are in a boat, in a storm, in the dark, and they're scared. They have forgotten the miracle of God in the storm of the dilemma. They had the lesson on the mountaintop but forgot it in the laboratory. In the dilemma, they forgot the Deliverer!

Travel Tip:
In your dilemma, direct your thoughts to follow the crumbs that fed the multitude. That path leads to the mountaintop.

That night, in the storm, the disciples looked up and guess who they saw strolling to them on top of the water? The Lord Jesus Christ. The Bible says, "They were frightened."

We get kind of sanctimonious about that. We say, "Oh,

it would be so sweet to look up and see Him coming."

Would it really? They were in a storm. Yes. They were scared. Oh, yes. But I think they caught on to something that we in the believing community occasionally forget. That Man walking on water has *full authority*! When we see Jesus coming to us through the storm, He is Lord. He has not come to take orders. He *has come to take over*.

It isn't always easy to turn the boat of our dilemma over to Him. He may not honor our idea of how to resolve the dilemma. He may expect our submission just at the time we plan to exercise our authority! It's not always easy, but it's the only way out of the storm.

Jesus called out to them, "Don't be afraid; it is I." I believe we scare easily because we know so little about Him. We know a lot about the storm. We might even know a lot about the boat. But until we know more about Him than we know about the dilemma, we're not going to know what it's like to enjoy the trip.

How can we know God better than we know the dilemma? By fellowship with Him *between* and *during* dilemmas! He is teaching us each day. He is preparing us through Bible study and the experiential appropriation of His principles. What we learned on the mountaintop we can *know* in the boat! We can know Him. Then we know how He can comfort us. He said, "Don't be afraid; it is I."

The disciples finally did the right thing. They were *willing* to receive Him into the boat.

Do you have a dilemma? Is there something beyond solution that's just sitting there on your agenda? I'd like to suggest that you give your dilemma to the Lord. It isn't always easy to relinquish a dilemma to Him. He may not handle the storm to your choosing. But He alone is Lord of the storm. Lord of the boat. Lord of the fishermen.

A woman asked me to pray with her for her husband.

He wasn't the Christian she wanted him to be. He didn't serve her Christian image as she wanted him to serve it. We prayed together; then I detoured a bit from honest petitioning. "Lord, make of this man what You want him to be. If You choose him to be a missionary, prepare the field, even as You prepare him. If You choose him to move to Mongolia and become . . ."

The startled wife tugged at my arm. "No," she said. "I don't want him to become a missionary . . . just a deacon."

I was wrong to misuse her prayer request, but there are times when we need to release our requests to God's will.

Once the disciples were willing to receive Jesus into the boat, *immediately* the boat was at land. I've learned something, in flight, sometimes with my claws out and eyes wide with terror, not knowing where I'm going, but just that I'm going to get there too fast. I can claim one incredible principle: When Jesus is Lord of the dilemma, He'll get me where I'm going. In that assurance, I can enjoy the flight.

Travel Tip:
Turn your dilemma over to God before your
boat turns over in the storm.

The Dilemma of Dilemmas

As usual, I seem to be always reminding myself of this principle. As I write this book, I'm constantly fighting two dilemmas.

First, I'm sure that it ought to be easier to put my thoughts down on paper. Somehow, my mind becomes congested by many different desires for the book. My thoughts are like cars sorting themselves out for a freeway exit. I want to address the feelings of anyone who might read this. I want to encourage each person and become a channel through which that person can experience comfort and then correct any errors in travel. I want to speak of heavy theology in a lighthearted way. I want people to like the book. Oh, yes, one other little thing: I want the book to be reasonably good and sell reasonably well. All these "want to's" tumble over each other vying for priority.

I try to exercise the discipline I use to correct my stammering tongue: orderliness. *One at a time now,* I tell my thoughts. *You can't say everything at once.* However, the thoughts that get pushed back get angry and leave! When their turn finally comes, I've forgotten them. I cajole them to return. I plead with them. I offer them bold type and triple spaces. Still they hide from me.

My second dilemma is the high cost of true communication: personal vulnerability. Maybe I need to stop a while and take my own advice to turn my dilemma over to God before my boat turns over in the storm.

It became much easier for me to do this once I truly understood a little verse: "The refining pot is for silver and the furnace for gold. But the LORD tests hearts."[5] This thought startled me at first because I didn't understand it.

Every time I would read anything about God's testing, I would get scared. I saw Him sifting through me and saying, "Well, this is garbage, this is garbage, this is garbage," and dumping all of me out. It frightened me. I kept looking at that verse. Finally, it occurred to me. Why is God doing the testing? Look at the verse: "The refining pot is for silver and the furnace for gold." What is the purpose of the refining pot? To find garbage? No! To find *gold*! Isn't that marvelous?

God says, "I am moving in your life because I know what I put there. *Gold.*" Isn't that incredible? When I go through difficult times and am frightened, I think, *Now He's going to find me out*. Well, there's nothing to indicate God has any doubt at all as to what I am. (Have you ever tried to protect God from knowing what you are? You pray other people's prayers; you confess other people's sins, just to cloud the issue so He won't know what you are. He knows what you are.) God looks at your life, where it is right now, and He says, "I placed gold in that life, and I am out to bring it forth."

Prophets in the Bible often had the difficult job of telling people when they were violating God's commandments. The prophet Jeremiah warned the people of Judah, a people who had run away from God and had gone through all kinds of garbage. Yet Jeremiah still prophesied, "God says to you, 'If you will extract the good from the rubbish, then you will be My spokesman.'"⁶ That excites me. Some of the things that are going on in my life are rough. Sometimes I'm going through things I can't understand. But God is in there, making known to me the rubbish, so that I'll bring forth the gold. And by that means, I will be, even me, *God's spokesman!*

With this viewpoint of my dilemmas, it is easier for me to turn my problems over to God. Maybe the reader and I need to stop and do just this. Maybe it's time for both of us to tune out our voices and hear the Lord's. "Hush and know that I am God."⁷ Amen.

SEVEN

Remember, If the Traveler Is Redeemed, the Trip Is, Too

We've looked at several travel tips. We've considered process, personhood, and problems. We've double-checked our luggage tags. Now, what about productivity? Can we, in flight, set our sights for productivity with any reasonable thought of realizing it?

Yes! Most certainly! God not only calls us to be productive in flight but directs our attention to the exclusive area for its realization. And then, as if those directions were not in themselves enough to soothe our doubts about personal accomplishment, He gives us the specific recipe for certain productivity.

THE CALL TO PRODUCTIVITY

As I looked to Scriptures to specify each person's call to productivity, I was astounded. What I sought was a principle to share. What I found was a principle to claim!

God's whole Book is a call to productivity. From God's first words to Adam in Eden's garden through the new song sung before the throne in Revelation, we are called to productivity. The fact of the call is clearly evident. And once we realize *that* it is, we have to consider *what* it is. What is the purpose of man? To glorify God. What does it mean to glorify God? To make Him known.

For that reason, Jesus Christ prayed in a garden, called Gethsemane, across the Kidron River from Jerusalem, "Thy will be done. Thy will be done. Thy will be done." The gospel of John gives us what may well be the most intimate conversation ever recorded. Jesus, the Son of God, cried out to God the Father, "Glorify Your Son, that Your Son also may glorify You."[1] Though my heart beats in a whisper whenever I think of it, this precious prayer phrases the purpose of the believer's clear identity. "Father, let my identity be known that I may make Your identity known. Let it be known whose I am that I can make known who You are." This is productivity: to glorify God.

THE AREA FOR PRODUCTIVITY

The proper and exclusive area in which we can be productive is outlined in the New Testament. "But thanks be to God, who always leads us in His triumph."[2] I used to think that verse meant *sometimes*, under very special circumstances, when my dial was set to religion, and when people and circumstances were perfect. But the verse says *always*. "But thanks be to God, who *always* leads us in His triumph in Christ, and manifests through us the sweet aroma of the knowledge of Him." Where does that happen? What obscure arena allows us to glorify God? The Bible says, "In every place." In every place, we are to make God known. Sometimes, when we think that we are in the worst possible place, that may be the very place we can most clearly manifest His glory.

My husband gave me a typewriter, a wonderful Italian typewriter, but it tends to make the same spelling errors that my old typewriter made. Some time ago, I tried to change the ribbon. I fussed at it. I punched little buttons. I hit the spools a couple of times. The ribbon wouldn't go in. I thought, *Well, since I've tried everything else, I'll look at the instruction book.*

So I got out the manual and opened it. I looked at those strange Italian words, and I remembered when a friend and I were preparing for a tour of Europe. We decided that she was going to learn to speak French and I was going to learn to speak Italian. I got as far as the first language record and stopped. The only thing I learned was how to rattle off about nine Italian names, which didn't come up in the directions for my typewriter.

I threw the book down, and when I did, I found that the back section of it was in *English*. Eagerly, I began to read the instructions. I understood the Italian better, but I still couldn't figure out how to change the ribbon.

I was so discouraged. Then I found a fold-out page in the back of the book. I could recognize right off that it was a picture of my typewriter. I looked carefully and noticed a bunch of little numbers. I knew that I wasn't supposed to paint them, so I figured that maybe that had something to do with directions. If my typewriter looked like that illustration, I was in business!

I recited the directions to myself as I studied the illustrations. "One little spool goes under the first little gadget." I did that.

". . . and then goes around the little thing that thumbs out to the side." I did that.

And then, *according to the picture*, the ribbon came up, around, and followed through three little bumpy things.

It went inside this one, came over here, and went inside that one and around the back of the other, and then, *according to the picture*, it came back around to fit onto a little spool. I did that.

I tapped the spool, and it went into place! It was marvelous. By following the directions and that illustration, I could get my typewriter to work.

What in the world is a Christian? An illustration, just like that picture of my typewriter. If the world wants to know how God's principles work, it can look at the believer. *There's* the illustration. In every place, in the dilemmas of our circumstances—in the hurts, in the confusion, in the discipline, and even in the questions—we are to make Him known. Where you and I are right now, we are to make Jesus' true character known.

That isn't always easy. It isn't easy even to write about it. Sometimes, making Him known in His true character means allowing the illustration of His discipline. I know what it's like to live out the principle of cause and effect— to have in my life the result of decisions and actions that weren't aligned with God's will. You may have cried out, as I have, "Oh, God, deliver me from this disciplinary pig sty, and I'll promise to make You known."

Travel Tip:
Make Him known in the pig sty, or you'll never make Him known.

A lot of runaway Christians don't know God has provided a means by which they can be restored to productivity, right there in the pig sty: the confession of sin. *To confess* means "to agree with." When my attitude toward a particular sin is God's attitude toward that sin, I am in agreement with God. By the practice of confession, I am restored.

Confession Equips You to Move Out of the Pig Sty

Confession is not a flippant matter because God's attitude toward sin is not flippant. He sent His Son to die on the cross for our sin. That is not casual. Confession does not imply a lip service that has no intention of practicing obedience the next time. God did not offer us phrases; He offered the blood of His Son.

In the early years of the A.D. Players, I was working with a group of young people some of whom were not Christians or were Christians who had wandered from their faith. I was eager to make the principle of confession[3] clear to them, so I included it in many Bible classes. One afternoon we traveled in a rented school bus to a church about an hour and a half from Houston. I had handled the details of this booking, in which I asked that a host meet us at the church at a particular time, that a stage be set up and ready for our preshow rehearsal, that a lighting crew be waiting with complete equipment, and that—very important—a meal be ready for our troupe prior to the performance.

When we arrived at the church at six o'clock, a few minutes early, we found no one there to meet us. Still we began unloading the bus. As the hour of the evening's performance drew nearer without our host's appearance, we got a late-working janitor to let us into the church auditorium. It hadn't been arranged as specified in our correspondence. We interrupted a deacons' meeting to find the way into the basement where platforms had been stored. We contacted the high-school drama teacher who made her stage lights available to us. By the time the audience began to arrive, we had a stage ready, lights in place with one very nervous janitor manning the spotlight.

My cast was tired, hungry, and looking to me for leadership. I was tired, hungry, and furious! The auditorium quickly filled with ticket-holding teenagers, and our cast changed into costumes. Suddenly, the smiling host entered with a small entourage of friends. He asked if everything was in order, and I answered that nothing was in order. He never stopped smiling. "I'll bet you run into this kind of thing all the time," he said. "But we all know the show must go on!"

I exploded with more show going on than he had ever imagined! I told him exactly what I thought of the whole situation, pointing out the deficiencies in a manner Lady Macbeth would have found appropriate. I let him know that "my" company could not be treated like that. My company required certain conditions: a host, a stage, lights, and a meal before they performed. But my company was well aware that the show must go on for that audience filled with teenagers, and the show would go on unless my company fainted from hunger.

Fortunately, my company was so enthralled by the drama of my reaction that they forgot hunger and weariness. They stood in awestruck silence as the young host withered down to his smile like the Cheshire Cat. The pastor, drawn by the commotion, now stood waiting in the doorway. A few audience members, who couldn't find seats, quickly decided the best show was backstage and gaped at me like bystanders for a news-on-the-street television interview. Once I finished, the silence was interrupted only by the pastor mumbling something about sending out for hamburgers. I eloquently vetoed the idea, saying the evening's show was starting immediately.

Another silence.

The host cleared his throat twice and said, "I'm sorry. We appreciate your willingness to perform anyway. Before we begin the show," he said, looking warily at me, "will you lead us in prayer?"

Everyone bowed their heads. My jaw dropped to my choker pearls. "Lead us in *prayer*?" I was so "out of fellowship," I couldn't follow them in prayer, much less lead them. The silence joined my cast in holding its breath. I knew I couldn't pray for the cast without getting myself back in fellowship with the Lord to whom prayers proceed.

I bowed my head. My voice had exhausted its bombasticity as I, in front of God and everybody, confessed my sad state. "Lord," I mumbled, "I have just lost my temper and vented personal anger and peevishness. I never inquired why this situation occurred or gave any consideration to the feelings of others. I was mad because 'my' company didn't get first-class treatment. I would like to pray for them and for this opportunity to offer Your gospel to five hundred teenagers through the medium of entertainment. Please forgive me and hear my petition for the show."

Then I prayed for the audience, the cast, the janitor working the lights, the host, and the pastor. At my "Amen," I was so embarrassed I couldn't face any of those on whose behalf I had just faced God. I went up to steady the janitor's trembling hand and click what switches my trembling hands could handle.

Our shows vary in their format since we have approximately thirty scripts from which to choose. That evening we presented a variety of material interspersed with music, ending with a play about Jonah. We've found that laughter makes us all vulnerable. Although our audiences laugh with us at a somewhat sanctimonious preacher who refuses God's direction to go to Nineveh because he is "Head of the Home Mission Board," the price of disobedient action and attitude is distinctly heard. The show, as I remember, was wondrously effective. The pastor offered to treat our cast to dinner at a nearby restaurant, and after mumbling my apologies, I started my car to drive home alone.

A young man whose interest in matters of God was minimal, but had joined our company for theatrical training, hailed me at the end of the church's driveway. I loved him. He was honest in his disbelief and equally honest in his questions.

I rolled down my car window, and he filled the space with his serious face. "We had a good show tonight, didn't we?"

I answered a brusque yes, uncomfortable in his gaze.

"You want me to drive back to town with you?" he asked.

"No, Bob, I'll be fine," I said

"Well, drive carefully." He began to pull away from the car. "By the way, you've been teaching us about confession. Tonight I saw how it works. Thank you."

By the grace of God, I had been productive *in that place* of discipline.

Years later, I listened as Bob turned his life over to Christ, but his life hasn't been lived comfortably in His palm. I have been told his feet no longer seek the path of the Master. As I pray for him, I know he saw how the confession of sin works. Wherever he is, I know that he is a believer. Perhaps people are watching him, as my cast watched me that night, to see what a Christian does when he is "out of fellowship." I've learned that "Forgive me" is not so hard to say, even in front of a crowd of people.

Some of you may be reading this book in the dim light of the pig sty. Runaway believers, wondering why you can't help those you love or why you can't illustrate God's love. You may have said to God that you'll praise His name just as soon as you get your life back together. Hear this painful principle.

Travel Tip:
Praise God in His discipline. Get right with Him through confession of sin or your life will never get right.

What in the world is a Christian? An illustration. In every place, to make God known in His true character. If you're not in the attitude of praise, correct the attitude. That correction may be the very illustration the world around you needs.

It's easy to give God glory in success. But we can also give Him glory in failure, defeat, the ashes of a broken marriage, the embers of a fiery misadventure, the sickening realization of personal error. The world is made up of people who know a lot about despair. But they don't know how to get out from under it. Some dilemmas are caused by wrong personal choices; others have no reasonable source in personal error. What is needed is an illustration from a Christian in dilemma. Don't deny the dilemma its holy opportunity.

Options Available After Mistakes

All people make mistakes; that goes with the fabric of our humanity. The question is, How do we deal with our mistakes? Perhaps the most popular option is to blame them on someone else. This is so easy to do that it scarcely gets credit for creativity. A more artful way to accomplish the same result is to respond with a diversionary tactic that focuses on an error totally unrelated to the one you have made. The final way is too rare: Admit your mistake.

Picture these options as though they were scenes from a soap opera, "One Time at a Day." The cast: husband and wife. The place: the foyer of home sweet home. We will explore diversion, denial, and admission.

Scene I: Diversion

HUSBAND: (entering) Who left the key in the front door?

WIFE: (who knows she left the key in the front door) Did you call your aunt?

HUSBAND: (with keys in hand and blank of face) What?

WIFE: Did you call your aunt?

HUSBAND: No, why?

WIFE: (with a sigh) Oh, no! You said you would call her this week. (taking keys from her husband) That poor lady sitting there all alone. (holding keys behind back and moving away from door) You should be more thoughtful of others. (dropping keys into straw kangaroo in corner of foyer) Oh, well. Don't worry about it. You can call her tomorrow.

Have you ever seen anyone play such a scene before—or played it yourself? I doubt that the husband has really been fooled, just sidetracked for a time. Certainly, God frowns on such dishonesty.

Scene II: *Blatant Denial*

HUSBAND: Who left the key in the front door?

WIFE: What keys? I don't see any keys! You're trying to trick me. (half fainting against straw kangaroo) I can't believe you would do this! (weeping into dust cloth) My only hope is that this is your idea of a joke. If so, we can go on with dinner and never mention it again.

This trick doesn't fool anyone, even for a moment. Sarah Bernhardt would have trouble making such a scene work. Another way is to overplay the incident.

Scene III: *Denial—Overplay*

HUSBAND: Who left the key in the front door?

WIFE: Oh, no! (gasping in horror) I did that! (grabbing straw kangaroo to heaving bosom) I am not fit to be your wife. I have jeopardized your life and the lives of all your employees. (weeping into dust cloth) Why did I do such a thing? Why? WHY? I have failed once again. I don't do anything right. (returning dust cloth to straw kangaroo) It would have been better for you if we'd never met. (returning straw kangaroo to floor and smiling piteously) Forgive me for the hurts I've caused you. I'm going to my room. Enjoy your dinner. I must have time to think. (exit with drooping shoulders)

The simplest way to deal with mistakes is to admit them—confess, accept their consequences, and go on from there.

Scene III: *Admission*

HUSBAND: Who left the key in the front door?

WIFE: I did! I forgot! I must remember to be careful about that.

Even the straw kangaroo applauds!

In real life the proper applause for the confession of sin or admission of error is sometimes missing. But then, life is not lived in the spotlight or under the watchful eye of director, makeup crew, coach, and camera. We can always be sure, however, that God accepts us in our confession.

Man is not always so compliant. And we usually have a little trouble forgiving ourselves. It is still simpler to admit mistakes and move toward correcting them, whether another person accepts our apology or not. (Incidentally, and contrary to popular theories, the previous scene's script is equally applicable with the roles of husband and wife reversed.)

Lest anyone think Christians are to illustrate God's principles only in times of stress and distress, let me remind you we are to illustrate Him in every place. In places of joy and ease, in places of love requited as well as unrequited, in victory parades, and in the blushing delight of a compliment. Wherever you are, that is the place and the time for making God known. Sometimes I falter because I try to do what I'm not assigned to do.

Some time ago, I was working in Christian theater and was very eager about working with various areas of Christian drama, but I was becoming less active as an actress. I thought, *Lord, I'm beginning to want to act again. I don't want this to be a problem for what You want to do in me, so I'll give it to You. Lord, if You want me to act, open an opportunity. If You don't, please, God, take away the appetite.*

Later, a friend called me and said my name had been submitted for a new movie. I couldn't believe it. At my office the next day, a very pleasant voice on the phone said, "Mrs. George, I'm calling you from our Burbank studios. I'm the producer of World Wide Films."

"Who is this *really*?" I answered.

"This is Frank Jacobsen, and I'm calling you from Burbank, California," the voice said.

"Oh, Tom, you can't fool me; I recognize your voice."

Mr. Jacobsen was very patient. He said he wanted me to send World Wide a photograph and a résumé so they could consider me for a part in a new film. Later, World Wide asked me to fly out for a screen test and an interview. I talked with the director, Jimmy Collier. I had a screen test, and Jimmy said they were considering me for the part of Katja in the film *The Hiding Place*.

Several weeks later, Jimmy called and asked me to fly back out for another interview. I agreed, of course, and then asked, "Have you cast the role of Corrie ten Boom yet?" because I knew that they had hired Julie Harris to play the part of Betsy, Corrie's sister, and had cast Arthur O'Connell as their father.

"We think we have," he answered.

"Oh, Jimmy, tell me. Who will it be?"

"You."

I arrived in California forty-five minutes before the plane did! I was to play the part of Corrie ten Boom in the film *The Hiding Place*! I was thrilled. . . .

And I was terrified. I had never been in a major film. I'm a stage actress. I would be playing the role of one of the most beloved women of our time, who, by the way, would be on the set watching me play her.

I couldn't understand how in the world this had happened. God had answered my prayer far beyond my expectations. Then people began to assure me that I was in the film so that I could lead others to the person of Christ. "You're there to witness," they said.

I thought, *All right, this is what I am to do.* I went to England with the group, and I kept thinking, *When I complete the testimonies I am to give, the real actress will come to replace me, and I'll go on home.*

I tried to validate my opportunity with testimony. Every time we read the script together, I was at a point of alert, ready to hand out the gospel. Anybody who asked

me any question about the script could get whole sermons from me. It became apparent that in my eagerness
to witness, I was irritating members of the cast. That hurt
me.

One particular night, the director talked to me. "Jeannette, you need to interact with the cast more," he said.
"That's where you'll find the best working relationship."

I felt awful. I had failed! Later that night, through many
tears, I said, *Lord, if You didn't send me here to witness to others,
what did You send me here to do?*

The answer was very clear: *to make a movie.*

So I focused on the work of the movie. It was amazing.
When I applied myself to my little piece of the mosaic—
the work at hand—God had the witness that He could
use. Apply yourself to your piece of the mosaic; let Him
work out the whole picture. Take a travel tip from Abraham.

Travel Tip:
Don't hold God to your plan.

Don't hold the wonder of our God, who has no limita-
tions, to your plan.

Abraham had a particular opportunity to realize the
significance of applying himself to his part of the mosaic
and letting God work out the whole picture. He didn't
have to know where he was going when God told him to
leave Haran, but he had to do what God told him to do.
Something difficult. Something tedious. Something I understand. He had to pack. I am the world's worst packer. I
will carry three times the luggage I need and have nothing in it that applies to where I'm going! I pack so many
options that I frequently leave behind what I meant to
pack in the first place. Packing is difficult. It occurred to

me that one of the reasons I had trouble packing was because I was trying to work out the *whole* picture instead of my assignment. Sometimes all I am to do *is* pack. Abraham obeyed. He packed and left the results to God.

There was a time when I was praying earnestly that God would let me have the part of Katja in *The Hiding Place*, the part that the producers first offered me. I might have said, *All right, God, I've been teaching Bible classes, and I've been good, and I've been going around doing the right things. It's time that you gave me what I want. I want that part of Katja.*

And God would say, *All right. I'll give it to you.* Then somewhere during the Millennium, I would have learned that God's plan for me had been the part of Corrie.

Don't hold God to your plan! It's difficult to release what we think is best, but true productivity is beyond our logic. Sometimes it's very painful. *God, here's my plan. Break it if You must. But do Your perfect will.* Then apply yourself to your part of the mosaic and let Him work out the picture.

Corrie ten Boom practiced this principle long before I knew it. As far as I can tell, there was no statement in the casting that the part of Corrie had to be played by a Christian. Corrie imposed no restrictions on that casting, but she did pray about it. The first night I met her, we got to talk together in the director's living room. I am told that afterward, once she was in her car, she raised her hands and said, "Praise de Lord. He has sent us an actress who knows Him. Hallelujah!"

THE RECIPE
FOR A PRODUCTIVE LIFE

Christ Himself has given us the certain recipe for living a productive life. Mrs. Earl Hughlett, whose husband is on the A.D. Players' Board of Directors, once told me of a young lady eager to know the secret of her friend's wonderful poppy seed cake. The friend handed her a sealed envelope with the mysterious directions: "Bake like any other cake but add poppy seeds."

Often directions for living the abundant Christian life seem to lack specifics. Not so. Christ has spelled out the secret of productivity for us. Two elemental truths *certainly* bring forth produce, He said, *certainly* bring produce: "I am the vine. You are the branches. He who abides in Me, and I in him, he bears much fruit. For apart from Me, you can do nothing."[4]

Don't Look for Immediate Results

I'm not very good with growing things. My plants don't react like plants are supposed to. But plants grow for my husband. When he goes out of town, he leaves little notes in the plants: "Do not water this." "Do not feed this." "Everything's all right." "Pray over this one."

Recently, he got some tulip bulbs. One of them was plumping out real good in the middle, but it was held at the top by little papery fingernails, and it couldn't open fully. I was curious to know what color that bulb would be. I didn't want to hurt it. I just wanted to be sure everything was okay. So I *very gently* peeled back one of those little fingernail leaves at the top.

I never did find out what color it would have been. It immediately turned brown!

You know what happened? I looked in the wrong place for evidence of growth. And when you look in the wrong place, you jeopardize the growth.

A lot of times in our Christian pilgrimage we're so eager for affirmation that our work has been productive, so hungry for instant gratification, that we demand evidence too quickly and from the wrong places. Jesus Christ said, "If I am comfortably at home in you, and you are comfortably at home in Me, you are bearing fruit."[5]

As a witness, I often expect immediate acceptance of my testimony. As a public speaker, I sometimes know engulfing despair because audiences don't respond as I had hoped. As a teacher, I frequently want my students to express learning with the fervent positives seen only in television commercials. My feelings may need that complimentary affirmation, but according to Scripture, I am to evaluate my productivity by my relationship with Christ. "If you are comfortably at home in Me," He said, "and if I am comfortably at home in you, you are bearing fruit." Instead of looking for external evidence, we need to look to our housekeeping: our relationship with the person of our Lord. To do so, each of us needs to ask an essential question: Can Christ be at home in my life?

Is Christ at Home in Your Life?

Christ has said that under some circumstances He will not be comfortably at home in us. For instance, in a life that countenances sin. Your lifestyle preaches your ethical moral standards, and Jesus Christ will not settle comfortably in that which is not aligned with Him. Neither will He be at home in a life that harbors bitterness and resentment.

I can still remember the day I found a verse in Scripture that said, "*Jeannette*, if you forgive others, I'll forgive you." I said, "Just a minute. I would like to go into that a little more thoroughly. Lord, that is an act of works, and forgiveness is by grace." (Have you ever tried to argue Scripture with God and realized that He says, "Never mind quoting it to *Me*, I wrote it"?)

"Lord, it is very difficult for me to forgive others," I argued. "I have a list of people I've not forgiven. I listed them alphabetically just in case I should forget one. I'm not about to forgive them."

He said, "If you forgive them, I'll forgive you."

And I said, "Lord, let me explain it to You. Some of these people did serious damage in my life. And I bear emotional scars. I'd love to tell You all the details."

The argument can go on and on if we're stubborn enough to ignore Scripture. The Bible clearly indicates, "If you will forgive others, then I will forgive you. But if you will not forgive others, then I [Jesus] will not be comfortably at home in your life."[6]

Some of us are confused because we think forgiving sin means condoning it. We are never to condone sin. Forgiving and condoning are two different actions.

In my internal argument with God, I said (as you may have), "Lord, I'm going to give it to You straight. I really feel I can't forgive them. Because, in the first place, You're going to forgive them, and if one of us doesn't hold on, they'll get off scot-free!"

Jesus said He will not be comfortably at home in a life filled with bitterness. When we maintain an unforgiving spirit, whatever the reason, we are saying to Christ, "I would rather have fellowship with bitterness than fellowship with You." We are to forgive, not because the object of our forgiveness deserves it, but because the object of our worship commands it.

I may not understand forgiveness, but I can say, "Lord, I'll take those people off my list. I give up my right to bitterness and anger. You can bless them. You can do wonderful things in their lives. I forgive them. I want to be right with You in You."

Productivity: God has called us to it. Productivity: God has assigned the area of it. In every place. Whether we are reading a book or teaching a Bible class or resting in the shade of a well-deserved vacation, *we* don't render the time productive. God does. Productivity: God has given us the recipe. We can render ourselves available through fellowship with God.

Travel Tip:

Don't wait until you land to get your act together. Look to your housekeeping—now and in flight!

✦✦✦

If we trust God for productivity, we can be assured that He will complete what He has begun.

God Will Complete What He Has Begun

God says, "I will complete what I have begun."[7] If you're worrying about the enormity of some task suddenly plopped down on your agenda, hear this great good news.

I saw the fact of that principle affect a young woman in one of my Bible classes. She had been brought to the class on a hospital pass. Around her thin wrist, she wore tape identifying her as a psychiatric patient in a local hospital. A friend had mentioned the class to her doctor, and he had okayed a visit saying, "Try it. Nothing else has worked."

As I taught, the young woman (I will call her Lenore) watched me with no response in her eyes. Her features graphed downward lines, and over them was the spotted brightness of makeup applied by unaccustomed fingers. Once in a while, she would look down at the open Bible her friend had placed in her lap. She was well dressed, but the outsized shoulders of her blue silk blouse spoke of weight drained from her body as expression had drained from her face. Once in a while, she would rub one curled hand along the blouse collar. Then the thin

137

hand, still curled, would hang awkwardly at the throat as though it were too weary to return to her lap.

I wondered why that poor, hopeless waif had been dragged from her hospital hiding place to sit without hearing in a Bible class. We were studying Philippians, and I referred several times to the sixth verse in the first chapter. At the closing prayer, I noticed she didn't bow her head but turned to stare at her praying friend as though she was fascinated by a dialogue she couldn't hear.

Afterward, Lenore was introduced to me and spoke with the politeness of a well-trained child. "I had a lovely time. Thank you for inviting me."

On an impulse, I hugged her and whispered in her ear, "Remember, God will complete what He has begun."

She stood within my arms for a moment, and I heard her raspy whisper, "Will He?"

"Yes," I said. "He promised. Philippians 1:6." And they left.

I learned from her friend that Lenore was a Christian who had turned against her children, husband, and pattern of life, and in a total breakdown she had been under hospital care for several weeks. Because of her violence, she had been restrained but now was able to stay in her room and make occasional visits to outside activities. She wasn't allowed to see her children, and there was no talk of her returning home.

The next week, I was surprised to see her back in class. Her friend said she had asked the doctor if she could attend again, and there she was sitting with unseeing eyes, as disinterested as one who waits daily at the same bus stop for an uninteresting ride to a meaningless home.

After class, I greeted her, and she said abruptly, "Tell me again."

"Tell you what?" I asked.

"Tell me again what you said."

"Do you mean what we studied today?"

"No, what you whispered last time," Lenore said softly.

I remembered that moment of our whispered exchange, so I could answer her, "God will complete what He has begun. He promised."

"Will He?" Her voice had no phrasing patterns; the words rolled past like box cars on a slow train. "Will He complete what He began?"

"Of course He will. He promised," I said and took her Bible from her hand and opened it to the verse. She didn't look at the page but kept her unblinking focus on me. "Look at it," I said. "See what it says."

She didn't look but closed her Bible and said again in a childish tremolo, "Thank you for inviting me. I had a lovely time." Her friend and I shared a despairing smile, and they left.

The next week, they were again at the class. This time, Lenore's eyes scanned the pages of her Bible and focused haphazardly as her friend pointed out the studied passage. I had just finished the closing prayer when Lenore came to me and said, "Tell me again what you told me. I can't find it in the Book."

I opened her Bible and pointed out Philippians 1:6 and had her read it with me. She said the words after me, a dry, dim shadow clinging to its image. When she looked at me, I saw a flicker of focus in her eyes. Her friend was smiling as she waited at the door. I watched them as they went down the walk, and I thought of the persistence of God and the faithfulness of a friend.

I was out of town the next week and didn't see Lenore and her friend the following week. Her friend called to explain that she had been out of town but would bring Lenore to the next meeting. This time Lenore followed the lesson in spurts of interest and then closed her Bible and stared at her hands folded over it. She looked better, as though she had done her own makeup with care. After the class, she came to me with her opened Bible, pointed out Philippians 1:6, and said, "Read it with me," and we did. I was crying, but Lenore was smiling.

So it went. Each week a little growth. Each week the verse read together. Each week a little improvement. Finally, she was released from the hospital and progressed to group therapy. She came regularly to class and began to look again like a lovely, vibrant young woman. One day her friend called me in tears. Lenore had suddenly reverted to her earlier dilemma. She had beaten one of her children, had run from her house and, when found, was taken back to the psychiatric hospital. We were bewildered.

Lenore's friend gave me her telephone number, and I called her. Once again, we claimed no hope but in God, no future but in His promise, and no assurance but in His Word. "God will complete what He has begun." This time the process was quicker; she knew the way. She was under an excellent doctor who encouraged her to return to Bible class and to make choices concerning her life with a socially acceptable, privately unbearable, alcoholic husband. I learned only a few of the details as I saw Lenore process past the high mark of her first recovery. Her children were again entrusted to her care. She began teaching school and resumed an active life with her children, which precluded our weekly Bible class, so I didn't see her regularly. I heard she was doing well, happy, and no longer under the pattern of debilitating depression. One day in class, I saw her. Lovely, at ease, eagerly following the lesson in her Bible.

After class, she came up to me and said, "I've wanted to find a way to thank you."

Thank me! Mine had been the privilege of watching

God at work in my friend. I knew she wanted to give me something, so I tried to express my feelings without rebuffing the spirit of generosity. "You owe me nothing, Lenore. I'm in your debt."

"But I wanted to do something in return for what has been done for me." She moved toward the row where she had been sitting. "Here is someone who is as I was. I brought her here from the same hospital where I was. Now, Jeannette, let's give her that verse."

Together, we sat beside a middle-aged woman who was staring blankly into a Bible opened to Philippians 1:6. She read the words with us, tracing them with the little finger of her right hand. Lenore hugged her and led her out of the room. A dramatic story but a true one. Oh, I've changed some of the details to honor the privacy of my friend Lenore, but the events in her life marked the effectiveness of God's purpose in her. God's grip is strong as I mentioned in chapter 4. He *will not let go*. He will complete what He has begun.

EIGHT

Read the Schedule Carefully

*O*n her eighty-eighth birthday, my mother said, "I like birthdays. They let me know you're still here." Some birthdays let you know how long you've been here with surprising clarity. One such mildewed birthday was my thirty-fifth. That was the year I accepted the fact that I would never play Peter Pan and that if I planned to segue from ingenue into leading lady without an abrupt transfer to character woman, I had better get to it.

The Sunday morning I reckoned with my thirty-fifth birthday dawned hot, gray, and muggy. I lay in bed awaiting the first telephone call greeting me with good wishes. None came, but I reasoned everyone thought it would be better to call during the afternoon. I had thought there might be some small tokens delivered on Saturday, but I had wrapped that disappointment in the usual problems of the postal service. I got up and dressed for church. Many dear friends attended my church, and I dressed carefully, knowing there might be special greetings extended in the early morning Bible class.

There were none. I knew my friends knew; we all kept track of each other's birthdays. Then I thought how embarrassing it might be if they had talked the preacher into some statement of birthday wishes *from the pulpit*. Maybe the flowers were in my honor! O*h, they shouldn't have done that*, I thought.

They didn't. The service was quite ordinary, and no one even patted my hand with simpering comments about agedness. Then I realized that they must be planning a surprise at lunch. We all usually ate together when we were not out of town working. I lingered after the service for someone to mention where we might gather, but no one said anything about lunch. They all seemed friendly but went off in different directions. I saw through their pretense. They knew where I ate when I chanced to eat alone on Sunday.

I walked to the restaurant near my apartment and thought I saw two friends hurriedly slipping in the side door. I stopped to check my appearance in the window's reflection and then walked in, primed to register surprise at the table full of laughing friends. There was no such table.

I ate in solitary grumpiness. With the apple pie, my attitude changed. They were waiting for me at my apartment! Of course! I didn't finish the pie but hastily paid the check and walked the half block to where I lived.

The mugginess of the day had begun a steamy shower. People scurried from canopy to canopy, but I recognized none of the scurriers. I entered the foyer of my building and climbed up the stairs. No giggles came from the hallway. No hugs welcomed me. No cards fluttered from my door as I opened it. I was bewildered but not dismayed. There would be some call—from someone. If my church friends were busy or had forgotten, others would remember. The young man I was dating would call from out of town. He wouldn't forget. He wanted me to marry him. He knew forgetting a birthday is not the best way to win a lady.

Certainly, a telephone call from my mother. I had sent her flowers. That should jog her memory. Nothing! No flowers. No cards. No telephone call. Nothing! I was to confront the assault of years alone. I wanted to call out from the window, "There is agedness here! Does anyone care?"

Birthday celebrations reckon that we are older. Without the celebrations, birthdays reckon that we are old!

By the middle of the afternoon, I accepted it. No one was going to pop out of the closet with lighted candles on a walnut cake. No one was going to arrive from out of town. My birthday meant nothing to anybody! I cried a bit in moist self-pity, regretting every card I had sent to others that year. I even wished I had back the enameled earrings I had given my friend Margaret on *her* birthday. Tearfully, I stammered a prayer thanking God for my health. (It is one of the few things one can enjoy alone.)

Then I became angry. I wasn't going to go down without a struggle. One person could still celebrate my birthday. Me! Still crying, I marched into my bedroom and changed into the boldest costume of youth I could find: a pair of shining pink stretch pants and a silver-gray sweater. I put on makeup, jewelry, high heels, and a blonde wig. Blondes may not have more fun, but they can certainly look cuter in misery.

I called out to myself in the mirror, "Happy Birthday! You are still young and will have a wonderful year. Happy Birthday, my friend!" I flounced into my living room, snatched up the Sunday paper, bounced like an ingenue onto my sofa stacked with pillows, and opened the paper. The date beneath the masthead shocked me. It wasn't my birthday. I couldn't believe my eyes! It wasn't my birthday! The paper blared forth the news that my birthday was Monday!

CHECK YOUR FACTS

I was horrified at my foolishness! I checked my calendar. The paper was right. I was wrong. I sat on the floor and laughed as heartily as my tight pink pants would allow. I had perpetrated a hilarious hoax—on myself. Even during the laughter, the principle was evident: One way to avoid misery is get the facts first. Emotions do not pander to logistics. Feelings do not check their own reasonableness. I've learned that misery has its own purposes, and generally when our pain has served its purpose, we dismiss it.

Travel Tip:
Don't let feelings exercise authority over your flight. Treat them to a good dose of facts long before you get out the sweet-smelling salve of self-pity.

You'll never recognize a wrong timetable unless you check the facts once you begin to sense something is wrong. Feelings, like fevers, are often symptoms that lead us to a proper diagnosis and eventual cure.

However, if the facts don't offset your gloom, check the reasons for your feelings. They may not deserve authority over your actions, as was the case for Jonah, the great reluctant traveler in the Bible.

CHECK THE REASONS
FOR YOUR FEELINGS

Jonah responded to God's call to be a foreign missionary by running away. His feelings about the decadent city of Nineveh got in the way of his obedience to God. He would rather have been a signpost for God's judgment than an invitation to His mercy. He would obey God's call only if Nineveh burned into stubble under God's wrath. Then he could wink at God amid the smoking embers of what had been a sinful city, and say, "Well, we fooled 'em, didn't we?"

However, in the whale's belly, Jonah saw his "calling" in a different light. (Don't we always? Whether it is in the pig sty or a sea monster's digestive tract, we prodigals tend to find our hearing greatly improved by the atmosphere.)

Back on dry land, Jonah wasn't slow in obeying his second call. He paused just long enough to clean his outsides from the whale's insides before he trotted off to Nineveh.

Jonah didn't have a committee because he couldn't take the time. He didn't have a billboard because he didn't have the means. He didn't have a song leader because he didn't have a song. All he had was a message, a judgmental attitude and, apparently, a very loud voice. "Yet forty days and Nineveh shall be overthrown!" he cried out, like some barefoot Paul Revere. He circled the wall Nineveh had built with the skulls of conquered people. He pointed to the temples where Ninevites honored debauchery as their religion. He bellowed his message in the face of obscenities scrawled on their buildings. He caterwauled his chants of judgment to crowds already wearing the scarred signature of licentious living. "Yet forty days—just forty days!"

And the people of Nineveh believed God and turned from their evil ways! So God repented of the evil He had said He would do to them, and He did not do it! Jonah's ministry met with great success. What joy that must have brought to the minister! But did it?

Not to this minister. The Bible says that this "displeased Jonah exceedingly, and he became angry."[1] Angry! Very, very angry! Why? Because God forgave the Ninevites once they repented of their sins. The only joy Jonah had in preaching God's word to Nineveh was in visualizing those pitiful pagans suffering forever in whales' bellies.

Jonah pouted, smoldering in sulky solitude under a leafy castor oil plant. His lower lip shaded the area where he sat as surely as the castor oil plant shaded his head.

God did not belittle Jonah's feelings or ignore Jonah's right to choose to be angry. He questioned the reasonableness of Jonah's reaction: "Is it right for you to be angry?" Is this anger a good choice? What is the reason for your feelings? Have you thought about that?

Actors know that feelings are a result. Most of an actor's technique focuses on contriving events to produce feelings. He questions "why" the feeling in order to portray what the character is experiencing. When the actor knows who the character is, what the character is doing, and why he is doing it, the how is a natural result (an overly simplistic approach to the wonderful complexity that is acting, but a basis for understanding God's dialogue with Jonah).

God's question is a reasonable one. Consider the events. Check the reasoning behind your anger, Jonah. Check the facts, Jeannette. Is anger, is revengefulness, is hostility, is withdrawal really the best choice? We choose to be angry. It doesn't happen to us. No matter how sudden the swell of anger, it is a product of choices. Those choices may have been patterned and programmed long before the event of anger, but the choices are in the process.

Don't wear out your feelings by misusing them. Emotions are wonderful gifts from God. They are not to be repressed, denied, devaluated. But they are also not to be miscued. There are times when anger is appropriate, but oh, there are more times when it is not! The book of Proverbs cautions us against the "man given to anger."[2] His ways are contagious and can entrap us. His anger is so deep that rescuing him from deep waters, or whales' bellies, will not do him any good. He must be rescued from his anger.

How did God rescue Jonah from such anger? God caused Jonah to experience a slight example of mercy. Jonah enjoyed the shade of a leafy castor oil plant, which protected him from the scorching sun. Then God "appointed a worm when dawn came the next day, and it attacked the plant and it withered."[3]

God's choices amaze me. He used a worm to preach to a prophet. A worm! I wonder how that little worm reacted to God's call. Did it curl up in a slithery ball, crying out its unworthiness? Did it melt away into a crack in the sidewalk whimpering, "I could never be so arrogant as to preach to a prophet"? No, worms are too smart for that. They obey God whether the clod of dirt that enfolds them seems to be upside down or right side up. Worms are aware of the value of process. They never miss a wriggle or drag whatever they use for feet. They obey God! That's why they are so useful in catching fish.

I can imagine that little worm, glistening and green, puffing out whatever he uses for a chest and chomping away at that leaf with all the gusto of anyone happy to glorify almighty God! And Jonah got the message. It took a whale's belly to teach him obedient action. It took the blistering sun to teach him the importance of mercy—to himself and to others.

There Jonah sat, drained dry in that searing heat. His

lips peeling and sore, his tongue dry and swollen, rustling like a broken leaf in the arid wind of his breath. His blistered feet drawn up under him so they might find some shelter within the lap of his robe. His hands, scalded by the sands, clenching and extending in pain. There was no lessening of the sun's rays, no winnowing of its intensity, no clouds, no shadow, no plant. He needed that plant to give him shade, even though that plant measured no more than one night's worth in the scale of eternity. Nineveh was just as important to God as that plant was to Jonah.

It's interesting that the city didn't long follow its course of repentance. Later, we learn the Ninevites resumed their wicked ways and were indeed destroyed. But God was interested in the few who might believe and be saved, the few who might breathe in the gospel regardless of what the world around them lived out. Yes, God was interested in the few who believed—and one of them was Jonah.

I wonder if Jonah may have found God's mercy a difficult principle to accept. Was Jonah unable to forgive the Ninevites because he still felt guilty for his own sins? Consider Jonah: a disobedient, runaway, judgmental prophet of God. And God heard Jonah in the whale's belly and delivered him! Could it be that Jonah's anger at Nineveh's deliverance was because his sense of justice was unable to agree with his own deliverance?

Are you at ease with God's mercy? Have you found it difficult to accept His love for *you*? If so, you will reflect that difficulty onto others He forgives. "Is it right for you to be angry?" Consider its source. Consider its irritation. Is it valid to lock yourself in the cramped corner of anger because you can't agree with the mercy of God?

The old adage—Look before you leap—is often offered as caution to those bemused by the influences of love.

I've learned that anger and malice and self-pity can make us just as giddy without the accompaniment of sweet bird song and words that rhyme with *moon* and *June*. A good clear look before you're livid would be a wise caution and a good travel tip for the Jonahs and the Jeannettes.

Travel Tip:
"Consider the feelings. How they grow. They spoil not, neither do they win. Yet Solomon in all his glory couldn't handle them."⁴ Is it right for *you* to be angry?

The answer is usually no. Yet emotions can be as refreshing as the morning rain. However, feelings tend to follow their own timetable. Laughter interrupts a program of great solemnity, tears spill through the split seams of structured smiles, and celebration stumbles awkwardly into times of grief. But emotions under God's authority surprise us with their alignment to His holy timetable.

I remember one morning when I had to ask myself the same question God asked Jonah, Is it right for you to be angry? Consider your feelings, Jeannette. How did they grow? As Lorraine and I sat at breakfast, our building manager called to say we were going to get a new carpet. For over ten years, I'd complained about our carpet. It was well worn, dreadfully faded, badly stained, dangerously uneven, and completely irreparable. Besides those minor negatives, I detested its color. Getting a new carpet should have been a joy.

However, as I glanced at Lorraine, placidly crunching his breakfast cereal, the thought of a new carpet wasn't immediately appealing. The samples were even then awaiting my inspection in the manager's office. The new carpet would be ready for us in three days. It wasn't likely that we would be ready for the new carpet! All our furniture would have to be moved across the hall to an empty apartment. Stacks of papers, magazines, and Horchow catalogues would need detailed attention. One hall closet would have to be tamed, trained, and trimmed before it could be measured, much less carpeted.

I was in the process of writing this book. I had a deadline to meet. I didn't have three days to play tiddlywinks with our furniture. The blessing of the new carpet had come at the worst possible time. How could God have made such a mistake?

A better question would have been, Why am I angry as well as rattled? Could it be guilt? Finally, I acknowledged a shadowy hint of mismanagement on my part. I had found it easier to complain about the old carpet than to make arrangements for the new.

With his second cup of coffee, I served Lorraine a flowing recital of my woes and worries. In characteristic fashion, he suggested some friends who would help move the heavy furniture and assured me everything would be much less complicated than my highly creative reaction had imagined.

After he left, I realized it wasn't the furniture that would take up my time. It was the stacks of "things." Stacks of books, small mounds of paper littering my desk, mail to be answered. And a most special cluster of cluttering: three baskets that had nestled in the far corner of our living room alcove for over two years. They held the letters and notes sent to us at the time of my mother's Christmas Eve death. Many times those baskets have called out comfort to me as I stumbled upon some aching moment of unscheduled mourning. I knew that I would have to sort through them. Their time had come. The episode of new carpeting directed me to a do-it-today address of those three baskets.

It was an experience of grief revisited, as I had suspected, but also of joy newly claimed. A numbness is part of young grief, a kind of protection from drinking more of its freshly brewed sorrow than we can tolerate. The time is not right. But two years later those hundreds of notes, which did not penetrate the cloud of fresh grief, comforted me in a clearer way as I sorted through the baskets. Friends I never knew were there, words wadded up with tears, phrases copied from letters that had offered help to friends in their times of hurt, soaring truths wearing the glorious stammering of inarticulate honesty. I feasted on fellowship, Christ's love spoken through His loved humanity. It was a new solace to me.

During those moments, I remembered my mother. Mother was a southern lady. Grimy with joyous work in the yard, she was still a lady of such style that even the newly planted pansies smiled. From her kitchen, she served an unenlisted army of teenagers hundreds of hamburgers, which paraded from that kitchen door like newly hatched ducks. Although the full bloom of arrogance blossomed in the adolescence of my high-school and college friends, I never knew any response to her courtesy but courtesy. I remember one crinkle-haired basketball player, slouched like spilled Jello over a porch chair, who expanded to his feet like a snapped rubber band when Mother entered. He smiled and nodded with all the grace of a nobleman in the presence of the Queen Mother. After Mother left the room, her newest ardent attendant stood in amazement at himself. He said, "My mother will never believe I did that," and he slouched back to spillage over the porch chair.

Music was that lovely lady's medium, and it surrounded her all her life. Bach, Chopin, and Liszt were as comfortable in their attention to her as that elastic young basketball player. She wanted me to be a musician. She tried to infect me with her talent, but I was immune. When she saw my fingers did not fit the glove of her music, she focused her enthusiasm just as eagerly on the inclinations of my chosen art. It never occurred to her that I could not do anything. In Mother's presence, losing hope was not an option. She loved me all my life and let me know it.

And so it was that I spent one whole and healing afternoon visiting with my mother's memory and with those who loved her and missed her, too. Love surrounded me that day. A surprising event. One forced on me by a timetable under a higher authority than circumstances.

In three days, and with a minimum of chaos, the new carpet was in place. The furniture took on a new dignity, and our apartment glowed with a warm elegance. The corners of the living room looked magazine-cover right without their clutter. The baskets were gone, but they had fed me well—in God's time.

On a gentle slope of Galilean hillside, twelve baskets full of food were left over. Don't worry about them. In God's unwavering economy, they will yet feed the multitude. Baskets full, waiting for their time to come. They carry the touch of the Master Baker who is, was, and always will be Himself, the Bread of Life. Those baskets full of bread, like His mercies, are fresh every morning.

Travel Tip:

You can trust God's timetable. A true expression of love is never wasted. Today, this day in your life, thank somebody, comfort somebody, surprise somebody with a note of "I love you." In His good time, God will see that it is a blessing—maybe even to you.[5]

NINE

Don't Forget Your Carry-on Luggage

Traveling is always cumbersome for me. I travel with so much in my hand, over my shoulder, and under my arm. Not wanting to waste a moment of each trip, I'm fully stocked for typing, reading, working, and worrying during every flight. I prefer a seat by the aisle and almost never dare look out the window!

One beautiful day while flying into Seattle, the pilot wing-dipped over Mount Saint Helens. I was swung from my rigid position by the aisle to the empty seat by the window. I could do nothing but look. There it was! A giant sundae that had blown its top! One gorgeous breathtaking view, and the plane resumed its usual pattern on to Seattle. I moved eagerly to the window seat and relished the splendor of the Northwest from the air.

Afterward, I realized that from my aisle seats I had been missing the view of our beautiful country. I had missed the Grand Canyon, the embroidered skyline of

New York City, the Washington Monument and other magnificent buildings in Washington, D.C., and the lightning bug convention that is the nighttime pattern of most cities in the United States. Since that incident of Mount Saint Helens, I always allow at least one scanning from my plane's window.

In the flights of life's pilgrimage, don't miss the view. Experience experiences. Don't let valuable occurrences slip by without the involvement of your participation. Take a risk and choose an occasional seat by the window. If you watch closely, each trip will have its own travel tip.

You and I have checked our itinerary, clarified our identification, chosen an excellent Guide, freed ourselves from improper luggage tags, but our travel plans aren't complete. Our carry-on luggage now needs attention. What must we have with us *at all times*? I offer five principles that can give you assurance *during* the trip.

1. HE IS ALWAYS WITH YOU

Last summer, the A.D. Players performed during Charles Swindoll's Insight for Living Alaskan Cruise. Lorraine and I had been graciously invited to join this wonderful venture on the SS *Rotterdam*. Our good friends Marge and Chuck Caldwell chose that cruise for their vacation, so on July 24 the four of us were on an airplane on our way to Vancouver, British Columbia, to join the cruise.

Suddenly, 30,000 feet above Denver, our plane began to sway and bump and tilt with the ominous creaking that always reminds me that the Wright brothers lived only three generations ago. I responded quickly. My hands became awash in clamminess while my facial muscles, disciplined to deny feelings of terror, hardened into what I hoped looked like a relaxed smile. The sugared nuts I had eaten with such pleasure cozied up to each other in one indigestible cluster. A hasty litany of flash prayers matched the staccato rhythm of my heart. One nagging thought hummed in my inner ear: I'*m not essential to the* Rotterdam'*s program. I will, in fact, be a guest, a minister without ministry, a missioner sans mission, a worker without a work order. Will God be inclined to hear my prayers for a safe flight when I'm not "about His business"? Isn't there a hint of effrontery in asking God to extend His holy protection to one whose approaching assignment may be of no more significance than choosing between fruit cup or smoked salmon for an appetizer?*

My questions reveal an interesting fallacy. Interesting, popular, but a fallacy! We trap ourselves in the gutters of superstition when we try to render ourselves validated by religious activity. The fact is that we don't really know when we are about a mighty work or when we are merely incidental to that work. God doesn't give us little colored tabs to mark the significances of our lives. For Christians, every day is a red-letter day because it has been soaked in the gift of God's love.

If I am holier at the podium of a speaking engagement than in the fruit and vegetable section of my grocery store, something is sadly wrong with my relationship with Christ (and my husband's supper is of questionable standard). Validity is expressed in obedience and availability and is the product of Christ's finished work, not ours. Our importance to God doesn't rest on what we do or our importance to other people. Christ said, "Lo, I am with you always." Is it possible that He truly meant *always!* Even vacations? Before the plane's path was steadied, mine was.

Travel Tip:
His fellowship makes your flight plan valid.
All His sparrows get His full attention.

2. HE ENJOYS KNOWING YOU

I learned this principle while resting on the sport deck of the SS *Rotterdam* during that Alaskan cruise. I had just gotten out of the pool when a young father and his two daughters entered it. The younger daughter, Michelle, who was about three or four, began to enjoy the vigor of swimming while her father held her securely midwaist and walked her through the water. Jennifer, the older daughter who was more advanced in the sport and equipped with arm floats, was paddling freely back and forth while her dad called out instructions: "Kick, Jennifer, kick. Cup those hands. That's fine!"

Testing her expertise, Jennifer called out, "Daddy, do you want to race?"

Daddy nodded that he did and, still carrying Michelle, joined Jennifer at the starting point. Michelle and Daddy were getting into racing position when Jennifer, eager to win, spurted forward with a great thrashing of little arms.

Immediately, Daddy and Michelle followed in the spray of Jennifer's backwash. About halfway across, Jennifer called out, "Go!" and glanced over her shoulder to see Daddy and Michelle already covering the gap between them.

The race was abruptly concluded! Jennifer's wails whipped wilder than her waves. "No! I hadn't said 'Go!' That's not *fair*!" Her flat hands beat out her anger. Her splayed fingers spanked the water as if it were a doll of severe disobedience. I was fascinated by the force of her fury; something about it was vaguely familiar. She bobbed up and down in the water like a pony-tailed cork. She screamed so loudly and so long that two men rushed out of the exercise room to see what was wrong, and a blonde masseuse appeared from the door of the massage unit.

Finally, Jennifer paused for breath, eyed her father through the spray of water, and awaited his response to her tantrum. Laughter! Laughter drenched in love without any hint of ridicule or judgment. His laughter bounced from wall to wall, erasing echoes of his daughter's fury.

Jennifer lowered her arms and treaded water in upright amazement as her father laughed. She heard the love, sensed its revelation, considered its lesson. Then she paddled to her daddy to laugh with him! He enfolded her in the arm not occupied by Michelle. Michelle laughed; it seemed the proper thing to do. The two men laughed and went back to the exercise room. The masseuse laughed and went back to work, closing behind her the door labeled: Quiet Please. Treatment In Process.

Allow God His laughter. He is not indulgent with our sin and does not consider disobedience cute, but He does delight in us. Like Jennifer's father, God often invites us to see our ridiculousness and deal with our error in the comfort of His uncompromising love.

I've been like Jennifer. I've struck out against innocent circumstances and accused others of my mistakes. I've called God unfair because He disallowed my cheating. I've assumed that my relationship with God was as tenuous as my relationship with some people I've known, who weren't able to withstand the revelations of my human error.

Not so! God provides an atmosphere in which the honesty of my admitted error can flourish—just because He delights in me and desires my fellowship. If I doubt this, I remember that "He delivered me [Jeannette] because He delighted in me [Jeannette]."[1]

Travel Tip:
Allow God the laughter of His love. Then cuddle up in the love of His laughter.

3. HIS LOVE RUNS DEEP

All of us seem to doubt love. That's why we're so elated when we find it—or when we see how deep love can be, as I did one Valentine's Day. Lorraine's present that year was a beautiful necklace, a slender gold chain with rounded gold streamers filling out its pattern. As I opened the jewelry box, Lorraine was grinning from ear to ear. I grinned only momentarily. My husband had thoughtfully placed an ad, torn from a magazine, in the box. The ad had caught his attention, and he had ordered the lovely piece of jewelry. It was a picture of the most tragically undernourished model I had ever seen! My husband followed my gaze and said, "When I saw it, I thought of you!"

Incredible! That lady's neck had the gentle shadowing of bones I no longer remembered having! He, Lorraine, a man of unquestionable integrity and generally good eyesight, saw *that* picture and thought of *me*.

"Put it on," he said.

I demurred, vigorously! "Not now," I said. "Let's wait and plan a special event. Like maybe a year after I've given up eating."

I suggested framing the necklace and displaying it in our hallway where it would pronounce his love for me to all who entered. He demurred. Instead, we decided on an evening in the not-too-distant future when I would wear the elegant necklace.

The next day I went to a dress shop nearby where a trusted friend worked. I showed her the necklace and the picture and explained that my husband had bought *that* necklace for me after looking at *that* picture. What could we do about it? We knew a raincoat would only help momentarily. (Even if it did rain, I would have to doff the coat when we went into the restaurant.) We looked at many dresses and finally found a lovely black one that would cover me as well as could be expected.

The day of the necklace's debut, I left the office early to have my hair done. Then I rushed home to comb it out. I labored at my makeup table. I put on all four seasons of makeup at once, hoping one would help. I put on false eyelashes. In my nervousness, I placed both on my right eye. My left eye looked nude, and my right lid was too heavy to open!

I got out the wonder dress and said to myself, *Take one deep breath now because once you get this dress on you'll not have another breath until you get home*! I put on the necklace. I dared not look again in the mirror. My hand trembled on the doorknob. I love my husband very much. I couldn't bear to see him disappointed. Then, gritting my teeth, my head held awkwardly high, I opened the door and entered our living room.

My husband turned and looked at me. I almost fainted in the silence. Then I heard him whisper, "Oh, honey," and I couldn't look him in the face. Would the strain of his false expectations be apparent? Then he spoke. Very clearly. "Oh, honey," he said, "it looks so much better on you than in the picture!"

No, my friends, that is not sentiment. That is love!

Years later, that necklace seldom reminds me of the

model and her picture. It more often reminds me of love.

God has a picture and a plan for you and for me. He has purchased at a great price a gift of gold more precious than any necklace. He offers it to us from hands scarred by its price. He wants us not only to receive it but to wear it in joy and confidence.

Have you lingered behind closed doors fearful that you wouldn't measure up to God's picture? Have you framed His gift and placed it on a wall where it proclaims a joy you do not claim? Receive His gift. Put it on! It is designed with you in mind. That is not sentiment. That is love!

Travel Tip:

Put aside reluctance. Put on God's gift and never take it off. It's a style just right for successful traveling.

4. HE EXPECTS YOU TO CELEBRATE NOW

Too often we spend our lives mired in "whens." "When I get married, I'll be happy." "When I have a house of my own (or a particular job or promotion), I'll be happy."

How ridiculous, since the "whens" may never happen, and God may have some surprises even more exciting than we could conjure in our wildest dreams. I was reminded of this on the day Lorraine and I celebrated our fifteenth wedding anniversary.

Lorraine arranged an anniversary dinner party in the elegant dining room where we had held our rehearsal dinner. As I sat by Lorraine and looked around the table, my heart was full of love for those people who had peopled the perimeters of our married life. I've grown up in their love, for many had been friends in the early patterns of my maturity.

Dr. Riley performed our wedding service. Mr. Kennerly escorted my mother to her seat where she, luminous as any bride, smiled upon our vows. Some of those friends had hovered with open arms when my father died and had been quick to share my tears at my mother's death. Those friends had broken with us the ring of bread we served at our wedding reception and had allowed us to live out the unique pattern of our marriage as though a traveling wife and an extended family of twenty-three players were the routine complements of a good marriage. They had taken our vows as seriously as we had and added their prayers to their witness. And I thought of spaces at our table: couples whose marriages became sad statistics in the tumbling aftershock of broken homes.

Not all marriages last. Not all Christian marriages last. All couples meant their vows as they knelt before a preacher and promised not to quit. None vowed to harm the other or bring misery to their children, which would damage the footprints of their children's children. None planned infidelity as they smiled at each other in the candlelight of wedding choices. None measured the joining of their lives as a parking place until they shrugged from cocoon to butterfly. They all pledged that the people they would become would cleave to each other. But they didn't hold the people they became to those vows. Not all marriages last.

I don't understand it. I used to have so many answers. However, that was *before* I learned to listen to the questions. I only know that marriage is an incredibly intimate undertaking. Strangely enough, we consider it when we are in love and therefore bemused out of our most rational logic. To my view, most people marry for the wrong reasons and divorce for reasons that are even worse.

I don't believe in marriages that have no points of stress. Ours certainly has no such idiotically idyllic pattern. We have dealt with problems and perplexities, spaces in our togetherness, incidents too personal to share.

Couples in love always think they know each other well. They never do. For instance, when I promised to love, honor, and obey, I didn't know that Lorraine hated brussels sprouts, or that he loved to read aloud from the paper I had just finished reading, or that he would omit the interesting parts of dramatic events at his office, or that he wouldn't be interested in the dramatic events in the lives of people neither of us knew but had taken up a lot of my time at a small retreat in Idaho. I didn't know that he wanted his laundered underwear stacked on the bed of the guestroom because only he knew the way to place these items in the drawer, or that he would become so hard of hearing he couldn't hear me point out antique shops along the highway, or that he could never think of a particular restaurant when he said, "Why don't we eat out tonight?" I didn't know any of those things.

When he trembled at the altar but promised to husband me so long as we both should live, he didn't know that I loved small boxes and darling little footstools, or that I thought it was fun to try out new recipes before I finished learning the old ones, or that I didn't like to be read aloud to, even if it was material I'd never read before. He didn't know that, to me, getting ready in ten minutes didn't count the minutes it takes to jot down the new idea for a play and the added time to decide not to wear the red dress because it takes too long to change purses. He didn't know that if I got up during the night to write, I would keep popping back into bed to warm my feet against his back, or that I would be a trifle miffed when he couldn't remember the name of my college roommate he has never met but who still asks about him in every letter. He didn't know any of those things.

Trivial? Oh, yes. And selective. But I have found that irritations are like feathered darts. The target has to welcome them or they fall to the ground. The pattern of the marriage decides what to do with the piercing of the darts. There is a mystery. Something happened at the altar where we pledged our vows. That something would hover like a protective mother bird over all the rustlings in our nest.

I don't understand it. I certainly wouldn't make seminar handouts of it. But at that anniversary dinner, my husband's profile cut as fresh a pattern of delight in my heart as it did when I first loved him. I didn't know that he would build a theater for the A.D. Players, or that he would search through countless catalogues to find the pattern glass I collected, or that he would arrange to have my mother's hair fixed for her sister's sudden funeral when I was out of town. I didn't know that he would pray with ease over each meal no matter where we were, or that he would put away his pipe forever without even arguing, or that he would encourage me to follow the promptings of potential, even though they meant he would have endless dinners alone and exorbitant long-distance telephone bills. I didn't know that I would never have to understand the pain of infidelity, or that he would call me beautiful when no mirror in the world would agree, or that he would protect me from the wind and rain and never ever lose the integrity of his authority.

At that dinner table on our anniversary, I celebrated my marriage. It has been good because of God, Lorraine, our friends, . . . and two bathrooms.

Travel Tip:
Celebrate in the now. Don't save all your joy
for memories.

One final principle has been very important to me.
Every once in a while God sends a spectacular happening into our lives. Playing the part of Corrie ten Boom was
such a happening for me. There can be a downside to
that blessing, I've learned, if we allow that happening to
overshadow the rest of our lives. We are called to live in
the present, not the past.

5. HIS PLAN FOR YOUR LIFE
IS NOW

During the weeks before we began filming *The Hiding
Place*, I was doubtful that I could handle the magnitude of
the assignment. Several Christians offered me the encouragement of a phrase from the book of Esther: "Who
knows whether you have not attained royalty for such a
time as this?"[2]

You remember the story of Esther and its account of
God's sovereign protection. Once upon a time, a long
time ago, there lived a great Persian king named Ahasuerus. He ruled over the empire that had captured Israel,
and in his kingdom there were many Jews who became
part of the culture and practice of Persia. One of these
Jews was named Mordecai, and he became the body-
guard to the king, stationed at the front gate where he
served diligently. He had a cousin named Esther, who
was his ward. Mordecai and Esther were not known to be
Jews. They practiced in secret what they kept of their
faith and may never have guessed that God would cause

them to proclaim in public what they merely confessed in private (not too unlike all of us, were they?).

Well, one morning when the sun was shining on the downtown streets of Susa, the Persian capital enjoyed a splendid parade. It was in honor of Haman who had been appointed Ahasuerus's right-hand man. Haman loved parades, especially when they were for him. In fact, he thought, in his evil, self-centered little mind, that all parades were for him. If they weren't, they certainly should be! On the day of Haman's parade, the procession filed through the city streets and up to the palace gate. Everybody bowed down to Haman. Even the trees waved their branches because the rumor was that anything that didn't bow down got uprooted! All Haman saw was a great sea of obeisance.

Until he got to the gate! Amid the crowd of those bowing bodies sniffling dust and praising Haman was one man who stood, unbent, unsniffling, and without a whimper of praise. It was Mordecai! You see, deep within Mordecai was his belief in the one God Jehovah, and he could not acknowledge another lord—especially the wicked Haman.

Many times, God makes His people known because they do not praise and pander to what the world deems praiseworthy and panderable. Many Christian heroes stand out in the crowd because they do not walk in the counsel of the wicked, stand with the sinners, sit with the scoffers, or join the booster clubs of worldly heroes.

You can easily imagine how furious Haman was. Mordecai had spoiled his parade, and if the news got around that only people who *liked* Haman bowed down to him, his parades wouldn't make it past his garage. Haman sent his henchpersons scuttling off to find out who Mordecai was and soon learned the who, why, and how of

167

Mordecai's refusal to kowtow. He was a Jew! Then Haman got the king to issue an edict to destroy, kill, and annihilate all the Jews. The edict was that specific. Destroy, kill, and annihilate all the Jews!

Haman had stumbled upon a common error. He made the mistake of picking on what seemed to be a weak people, not knowing that behind them stood the invincible God. God is a superior parent. He disciplines His children with always effective, and sometimes severe, methods, but any outsider who lays a finger on one of God's children learns the practical meaning of "the wrath of God."

Meanwhile, back at the palace, Esther had become queen. She had won a national beauty contest and been chosen by the king as the "Virgin Most Likely to Become Oiled and Spoiled, Scented and Contented." In the midst of all the lavish attention, no mention was made by Esther or anyone else that she was a Jewess. She was happily reigning as Ahasuerus's Number One Queen when her maids brought her a note from Mordecai who was sitting unhappily in sackcloth and ashes outside the king's gate. Once she learned he was wearing second-hand sackcloth, she sent him a new robe. She was such a compassionate queen!

Mordecai said thanks for the new threads, but that really wasn't the problem. He was somewhat depressed because he and all the other Jews were to be destroyed, killed, and annihilated. He suggested that Esther pop in on the king and plead for her people, the Jews.

Esther said that one didn't "pop in" on His Royal Highness. Her turn for wifely visitation wasn't imminent (in fact, the king had to call for her), and Her Royal Husband didn't know she was a Jewess. Under the circumstances, it didn't seem to be a good time to bring up that matter!

It was then that Mordecai told it to her straight. He

said, "If you remain silent at this time, relief and deliverance will arise for the Jews from another place and you and your father's house will perish. And who knows whether you have not attained royalty for *such a time as this*?"³

The rest of the story (Esther's obedience, Mordecai's promotion, Haman's defeat, and God's deliverance of the Jews) deserves a good reading of the biblical text. That verse in Esther affected my life before, during, and after *The Hiding Place*.

For *this* you have been brought into the kingdom. Many nights when the work was so hard I thought I'd never make it, I would whisper, "It was for this I was brought into the kingdom." It became my flashlight in the darkness, my beacon in the storm, my cuddle slippers, my bedtime sweet, my rallying cry. I thanked God for that verse.

Until I came home and the film was finished. All of a sudden, it was over. A year had melted like snow in the sunlight. The personal appearance tours were over; the awards were given and forgotten; the loud uniqueness of stardom was only a fading whisper, and it was for *that* I had been brought into the kingdom. *That* was over, and I was still here. *That* was past, and I was present. How could I live when the purpose of my life was finished, and apparently, I was not?

When I returned to the Scripture, I realized I had misunderstood the verse. Oh, my dear friends, it was never for *that* you were brought into the kingdom, always for *this*. Esther was created not for one event but for a principle put into effect in the continuity of her life. Obedience! Trust! Honesty! All in the immediacy of now.

I've known this principle for years, yet I frequently forget to take this piece of carry-on luggage with me (just as I forget one or two of the others). Thank heavens, my loving Father is kind enough to remind me, as He did when I was speaking to a Christian Counseling Ministries renewal conference at Trail West Lodge in Buena Vista, Colorado.

The lodge juts out over an incredibly beautiful valley and directly faces Mount Princeton. At the time, I was feeling sorry for myself, burdened with several personal and professional choices. I went out onto the balcony and cried out tearfully to God, my hands gripping the balcony rail and my head down in an attitude of humility and misery. "God, please direct me," I cried through my tears.

Right after that cry, I realized I had been whining, not necessarily praying, that request for thirty years! For thirty years, I had been asking God to initiate His direction upon Jeannette Clift George.

That day I almost heard God say, "Jeannette, how do you think you, a middle-aged Texas woman, got to the balcony of a cabin at Trail West, looking at Mount Princeton, where you are speaking to a conference of Christian counselors, if I weren't directing you? How else could *you* get *here* but by Me?"

Suddenly, I realized that for thirty years I had been whining for God to do what He had been doing for thirty years!

You know, if somebody asks me for help or advice and I'm qualified to respond, I'll give an answer. If the person leaves and comes back and asks for the same advice again, I'll patiently respond again. I can be very patient and loving with people. I understand them. I've been a person for a long time.

I'll hand out the same answer, usually in the same tone but a little more slowly and distinctly, when the question is asked a third time. The fourth time my lips will tighten just a bit; but by the fifth time the tightness will even be noticeable in my voice. But what if the question was asked for thirty years? What then?

I don't think I'd answer. But God did. For thirty years, I had been whining for His direction, and for thirty years, He had been guiding me unfalteringly. The one with the deaf ear was me, not God!

Travel Tip:

God's plan for your life is not past tense or hidden in the obscurity of the future. It is continuous. God's will is always current.

It is for *this* you have been brought into the kingdom: to live this day, within its circumstances, in obedience. To stretch out in the fact of His security and be willing to become. To celebrate His presence even in flight. God has a plan for you. It is current. Celebrate it! Now!

NOTES

Chapter 1

1. Romans 12:2 PHILLIPS.
2. Romans 5:8, italics added.
3. Taken from Romans 10:17 NASB.

Chapter 2

1. Exodus 3:11 NASB.
2. 1 Corinthians 15:10 NASB.
3. 2 Corinthians 5:17.
4. John 1:12 NASB, italics added.
5. Proverb 11:3 NASB.
6. Taken from John 17:9–11 NASB.

Chapter 3

1. Taken from Matthew 9:16–17 NASB.

Chapter 4

1. Taken from Jeremiah 29:11 NASB.
2. Taken from Isaiah 49:16 NASB.
3. Joshua 1:5 NASB.
4. Taken from Hebrews 13:5 NASB.
5. See 1 Thessalonians 5:24.
6. Taken from Exodus 6:5–6 NASB.

7. Exodus 6:6 NASB, italics added.
8. Isaiah 53:5 NASB.

Chapter 5
1. See 2 Kings 5.
2. Taken from Proverb 2:2–5 NASB, italics added.
3. See Matthew 13:24–30.
4. Taken from Proverb 30:15 NASB.

Chapter 6
1. See Numbers 13.
2. Exodus 23:30 NASB, italics added.
3. Exodus 16:3 NASB.
4. Taken from Numbers 13:32–33 NASB.
5. Taken from Proverb 17:3 NASB.
6. Taken from Jeremiah 15:19 NASB.
7. Taken from Psalm 46:10 NASB.

Chapter 7
1. John 17:1.
2. 2 Corinthians 2:14 NASB.
3. See 1 John 1:9.
4. Taken from John 15:5 NASB.
5. Taken from John 15:5 NASB.
6. Taken from Matthew 6:15 NASB.
7. Taken from Philippians 1:6 NASB.

Chapter 8
1. Taken from Jonah 4:1 NASB.
2. Proverb 22:24 NASB.
3. Jonah 4:7 NASB.
4. Compare with Matthew 6:28–29.
5. Taken from Hebrews 10:25 NASB.

Chapter 9
1. Psalm 18:19.
2. Esther 4:14 NASB.
3. Esther 4:14 NASB, italics added.